What's

Submission

Got to Do

with It?

What's Submission Got to Do with It?

Find Out From a Woman Like You

Cindy Easley

MOODY PUBLISHERS
CHICAGO

All Scripture quotations, unless otherwise indicated, are taken from the
Holy Bible, New International Version®. NIV®. Copyright © 1973, 1978,
1984 by International Bible Society. Used by permission of Zondervan. All
rights reserved.

Scripture quotations marked NASB are taken from the *New American
Standard Bible*®, Copyright © 1960, 1962, 1963, 1968, 1971, 1972, 1973,
1975, 1977, 1995, by The Lockman Foundation. Used by permission.
(www.Lockman.org)

Scripture quotations marked THE MESSAGE are taken from *The Message*,
copyright © by Eugene H. Peterson 1993, 1994, 1995. Used by permission
of NavPress Publishing Corp.

Scripture quotations marked KJV are taken from the King James Version.

Editor: Jeanette Gardner Littleton
Interior Design: Ragont Design
Cover Design: Garborg Design Works, Inc., Savage, MN

Library of Congress Cataloging-in-Publication Data
Easley, Cindy.
  What's submission got to do with it? : find out from a woman like you /
Cindy Easley.
    p. cm.
  ISBN: 978-0-8024-5288-7
  1. Wives—Religious life. 2. Christian women—Religious life.
3. Submissiveness—Religious aspects—Christianity. I. Title.
  BV4528.15.E37 2008
  248.8'43—dc22

                                                                2008024722

This book is printed on acid free recycled paper containing 30% PCW
(Post Consumer Waste) and manufactured in the United States of
America by Bethany Press.

We hope you enjoy this book from Moody Publishers. Our goal is to provide high-quality, thought-provoking books and products that connect truth
to your real needs and challenges. For more information on other books and
products written and produced from a biblical perspective, go to www.
moodypublishers.com or write to:

Moody Publishers
820 N. LaSalle Boulevard
Chicago, IL 60610

1 3 5 7 9 10 8 6 4 2

Printed in the United States of America

To Michael

Thank you
for your sacrificial love
and for encouraging me to step
out of my comfort zone.

I will follow you anywhere.

Contents

Preface

WHY IN THE WORLD would I write a book on submission? I'm sitting at my computer, thinking of the hate mail I'm sure to receive. I'm not someone to run toward conflict; on the other hand, I don't have any problem standing firm for what I believe to be true. So here I am writing a book I know will be considered controversial at best, adversarial at worst. Let me tell you how this started.

I was raised in a home with a quiet, subservient mother who waited on my father hand and foot. I vividly remember my father returning from work in the evenings. As soon as he walked in the back door, my mother would follow him into the bedroom, shut the door, and they would spend a few minutes talking over the day.

Mostly I remember hearing my father's raised voice. He often seemed to yell at her, but she never responded in kind. I determined at that time that I would *never* be like my mother. I loved her immensely, but I would never let a man treat me like that. Later, when I heard the word *submission*, I decided if my mom was submissive, I certainly would never follow her example.

The concept of submission didn't creep back into my conscience until I was married. I respected my husband, falling for him in part because I saw him as a stronger leader than I was. This was rare for me. I would have classified myself as a Christian feminist, but knew that Michael was a man I would be willing to follow. Somewhere along the way I was confronted with the idea of submission again. I didn't like it or agree with it, but the more I studied the Scriptures, the more I became convinced that God did, indeed, give us roles in marriage to adhere to. I was concerned that so many people misrepresented biblical submission, even those who touted themselves as biblical literalists. I expected the world to misunderstand submission, but thought those who taught the Bible from our pulpits should know better.

In our culture submission is viewed as a throwback to the 1950s and the days of *Leave It to Beaver*. Submission is represented as repressive servanthood, rather than a voluntary desire to empower a husband's leadership. Marriages that accept the headship/helper model are mischaracterized as one-sided, with wives who are "barefoot and pregnant in the kitchen," who have little to offer in their thoughts or opinions. A submissive wife is considered to be more like a Stepford wife than an intelligent woman who is capable of her own choices. After all, what rational woman would ever choose to follow a man?

As with many things in our culture, this view of submission has found its way into the local church's teachings. In recent times the church has faced debate over whether God ordained marriage to be egalitarian or complementarian.

In an egalitarian marriage, the roles of husband and wife are equal. In other words everything is fifty-fifty. Roles are defined by the couple, rather than by culture or even the Bible.

I have to admit, this view is more palatable than the complementarian view. After all, no one wants to be considered the "lesser" in a relationship. On the other side of the aisle is the idea of a complementarian marriage. This view states there are distinct roles in a marriage. The husband is the head of the relationship; the wife is the helper. Although the man and woman stand equal before God in worth, they have specific roles. They complement each other in these roles.

My goal in this book is to give us a practical idea of what submission looks like in marriage. We are all sinners, so submission is not easy. What does submission look like in a less than perfect marriage? Does God let us off the hook if our husbands don't love us like Christ loved the church? I have asked women in different situations, "How does this work for

11

you?" I want to get inside their heads and their homes, so we can all get an idea of how to practically apply this concept in our own lives.

But I have to begin with a discussion of God's view of submission and why it's such a hard concept to grasp . . . and live out. This I will do in the first couple of chapters. Then I will move on to the stories of real women, with real marriages, who have sometimes struggled with God's plan. By the way, I've changed some of the names and details of these women to protect their privacy.

I hope as you read these stories that you will gain a better appreciation of God's will in your marriage. I hope you will grow closer to your Savior and to your husband as you learn what submission can look like in your home.

What Was God Thinking?

"For my thoughts are not your thoughts, neither are your ways my ways," declares the Lord. "As the heavens are higher than the earth, so are my ways higher than your ways and my thoughts than your thoughts."

—Isaiah 55:8–9

I AM OPINIONATED. I am independent. I am strong-willed. I am not afraid to make decisions. I am happy to take leadership. I am confident. I am also ... submissive to my husband. To many women, this seems much like the confession of a person at Alcoholics Anonymous. You know, "Hi. I'm Cindy, and I'm submissive."

Even writing those words rankles me. If I am all those things I say I am—opinionated, independent, confident—why did God choose me to be submissive? What was God thinking?

IT ALL STARTED IN THE GARDEN

Let's look at the beginning. That's where it all started. Pick up a Bible and look at the very first book, the very first chapter, Genesis 1, where we read about God creating the heavens and the earth. Right from the start you can see that God created the world with order. God made light, and separated it from the darkness. He made water and dry land. Then He moved on to vegetation and plants and fruit-bearing trees. On the fourth day God created the stars and sun and moon. Then He created all kinds of fish and birds and things that swarm. On the sixth day God made animals and everything that creeps on the ground. And on that day God also created His crowning achievement:

God created man in his own image, in the image of God created he him; male and female created he them (Gen. 1:27 KJV).

Did you notice the progression? God brought order out of chaos. Our God is a God of order. But we can't stop there. Genesis 2:7 explains the creation of man and woman in more detail: "The Lord God formed the man from the dust of the ground and breathed into his nostrils the breath of life, and man became a living being."

After God created man, God gave him his work orders. God planted a beautiful garden, and placed Adam in the middle. Adam's job was to take care of the garden. And *then* God created the woman. God saw that it was not good for man to be alone, and fashioned a helper specifically designed to meet the man's needs:

The Lord God said, "It is not good for the man to be alone. I will make a helper suitable for him" (Gen. 2:18).

Now you may think, *Wait a minute. What's this helper thing? I don't like the sound of that at all!*

Frankly, I didn't either . . . until I understood what the word "helper" really meant. In our culture we tend to think of a helper as someone who is subservient. But in Scripture, the designation of "helper" is given to God Himself.

"Hear, O Lord, and be merciful to me; O Lord, be my help" (Ps. 30:10).

"Surely God is my help; the Lord is the one who sustains me" (Ps. 54:4).

These verses use the same Hebrew word for "helper" (*ezer*) as in Genesis 2:18. God is *my* helper. He is *your* helper. And I'm certain God did not intend for us to assume that being our helper puts Him in a position of inferiority.

So even in the garden, God created order in marriage. In Paradise, before sin entered the equation, God designated the woman as the helper of man.

BIBLICAL LINES OF AUTHORITY

We all live under authority. Scripture does not single out wives for submission. God has placed everyone in subjection to the government (Rom. 13:1–2; Titus 3:1). We recognize this authority in our lives and choose to obey it or suffer the consequences. We obey the speed limit, pay our taxes, and even keep our grass cut so we don't have conflicts with our federal, state, or local governments. We may complain, but we comply because we don't want to suffer the penalty for not following the laws of the land.

God has also established a line of leadership in our homes. Ephesians 5:22–6:9, as well as Colossians 3:18–4:1, describe this authority: Children are subject to parents, wives to husbands, and husbands to God. Additionally, God reminded slaves to be obedient to their masters as to Christ, which we can apply to employees today and their bosses (Eph. 6:5).

In both of these passages, the *reason* we are to follow these lines of authority is because, ultimately, we are doing it for Christ's sake:

Whatever you do, do your work heartily, as for the Lord rather than for men, knowing that from the Lord you will receive the reward of the inheritance. It is the Lord Christ whom you serve (Col. 3:23–24 NASB).

Even Jesus submitted to authority in His life. You probably remember the story of Jesus going to the temple with His parents when He was twelve years old. As Mary and Joseph left Jerusalem, they noticed that their son was not with them. As a parent, I can imagine their panic. They thought He was with friends or family, only to discover He was not even in the caravan returning to Nazareth. They eventually returned to the temple complex and found their son sitting amid the teachers. Scripture tells us that Jesus' maturity and spiritual understanding amazed those who heard His answers.

Apparently Mary wasn't quite so easily impressed. She gave Jesus a quick tongue-lashing, as any panic-stricken mother would, and took Him home. Luke 2:51 ends the story with these words, "And He [Jesus] went down with them and came to Nazareth, and He continued in subjection to them" (NASB).

Wait—what? Jesus, who had just wowed the teachers in the temple, was submitting to His parents. This is not some ordinary twelve-year-old. This is Jesus, also known as the Son of God, the Prince of Peace, the King of Kings, the Lord of Lords. Now, before you run to your twelve-year-old son and throw this verse in his face, reflect on how it applies in your own life.

If Jesus, who created the world, willingly submitted to His fallible parents, wouldn't it follow that wives should be willing to submit to fallible husbands? We might like to believe that God really didn't mean this when He assigned our roles in marriage. Or that He certainly must have changed His mind as He realized how progressive His creation had become. But God allowed His own Son, the sinless One, to be placed under the authority of sinful human parents. I have a hard time believing that God would allow Jesus to be placed in a submissive relationship yet let me off the hook just because I don't always like submitting.

17

Scripture seems to indicate that God likes order. We've seen it from the creation of the universe through the management of the family. God knows that His creatures function best with disciplined, organized lives. God didn't intend for our marital roles to be a burden to us. In fact, God gave us a mission: to be a living, breathing example for the fallen world. Our marriages are sacred, and our complementarian roles are a high calling.

A UNIQUE RELATIONSHIP

God continued His thoughts on marriage through the apostle Paul, in his letter to the Ephesian church:

Wives, be subject to your own husbands, as to the Lord (Eph. 5:22 NASB).

The first thing that strikes me about this verse is the little word "own." Wives, be subject to your *own* husbands. This is not a directive to every male/female relationship. This is not addressed to women in the workplace, nor does it even refer to how a woman treats her boyfriend or fiancé. The only man a woman should be subject to is her *own* husband. This is a relationship like none other. Although it might seem contrary to our expectations, a woman can function in a position of authority in the workplace while she still lives in a position of submission in her relationship to her husband.

Interestingly, the word "subject" comes from a Greek military term that means to arrange troops under the command of a leader. In nonmilitary terms, submission is an attitude of voluntary cooperation. I like that. It's something I can comprehend as I ask myself, "Am I choosing to voluntarily cooperate with Michael?" When I do, I am giving him the respect he longs for.

But read on. This verse also says a wife should be subject to her own husband, *as to the Lord*. For whatever reason, God chose to place the husband as the head of the relationship. When we refuse to accept God's design, we are, in essence, telling God we don't trust Him. At times, being willing to follow our husbands is certainly difficult, yet that is what God asks of us.

God will use your willingness to cooperate with Him and your husband to work in both of your lives. I have been amazed as I look back over my own life to see how this principle has repeatedly come to fruition. When I submit to Michael's leadership, God works in both of us. That leads me to wonder if I am hindering God's work in our lives when I'm not willing to submit to Michael.

Let me give you an example. Although I am pragmatic, I still tend to make decisions that satisfy my emotional bent. Michael, like many men, is much more deliberate in his decisions. He looks at the facts, weighs the possibilities, and chooses what he perceives to be the best option. It drives me crazy! He can take months to make a major purchase, like buying a car. I can do it in an afternoon. I don't really care about the best ratings or gas mileage or service record. I want the cute one. Obviously, it is to my personal advantage to follow his lead. The cute car isn't so appealing when it's in the shop . . . again.

God has wired our husbands to need our respect, just as we are wired with the need to be loved. When I willingly submit to Michael's leadership, I receive another bonus. He takes his position of leadership more seriously, realizing that I will follow. I expect Michael to listen to my desires, and my advice when I have more knowledge than he does on a specific subject. However, I've found over and over again that it is in my best interest to allow him to play the role that God gave him.

When we are willing to cooperate with our husbands' leadership, they stand taller, feel prouder, and become the men we know they can be.

A DIVINE PICTURE

Maybe you've heard that old saying, "You may be the only Bible that some people ever read." Perhaps that is what God intended in a Christian marriage, as described in Ephesians 5:23–27 (NASB):

For the husband is the head of the wife, as Christ also is the head of the church, He Himself being the Savior of the body. But as the church is subject to Christ, so also the wives ought to be to their husbands in everything. Husbands, love your wives, just as Christ also loved the church and gave Himself up for her, so that He might sanctify her, having cleansed her by the washing of water with the word, that He might present to Himself the church in all her glory, having no spot or wrinkle or any such thing; but that she would be holy and blameless.

What an awesome responsibility! When Michael loves me as Christ loved the church and when I respond in submission to him, we are a divine picture for the entire world to see.

This certainly makes our marriages appear different from the model the world is trying to sell! The husband is to sacrificially love his wife. The wife is to voluntarily cooperate with her husband in everything.

What if every Christian marriage lived by these principles? Our marriages would be divine! Our neighbors, our coworkers, and our families would all demand to know how to achieve such great marriages for themselves. And we would have the answer! We would be in the perfect position to share the love of Christ with them.

YES, GOD, I GET IT!

As I have chased the idea of submission through the Bible, one portion of Scripture was the final straw that convinced me of God's opinion on this subject:

Your attitude should be the same as that of Christ Jesus: who, being in very nature God, did not consider equality with God something to be grasped, but made himself nothing, taking the very nature of a servant, being made in human likeness. And being found in appearance as a man, he humbled himself and became obedient to death— even death on a cross! (Phil. 2:5–8)

Jesus Christ chose humility over pride. He is equal with God in all respects, because He is God. Yet He willingly left the throne of heaven to live as a servant on earth. Jesus took on hunger, exhaustion, grief, temptation, disappointment, and abuse from the very people He came to save. He voluntarily cooperated with God the Father in a plan that required His painful death on our behalf. He humbled Himself.

Humility seems to be an important character trait in God's economy. The Bible is full of Scriptures that reveal God's attitude toward those who are humble in spirit. This, more than any other argument, has clarified my thoughts concerning my role in the marriage relationship: "God opposes the proud but gives grace to the humble" (James 4:6).

Submission requires humility. I am a proud creature. I can't think of a better way for God to mold me in His image on a daily basis. When I choose to humble myself and respect my husband, placing myself under his authority, I can almost feel God whisper, "Well done."

Why Is Submission So Hard?

*It is better to live in a corner of the roof
than in a house shared with a contentious woman.*
—*Proverbs 25.24 NASB*

IN JUNE 2006, Lawrence Summers, the president of Harvard University, resigned his post after weeks of verbal assault from the faculty. Dr. Summers's egregious action was not embezzlement, moral deficiency, sexual harassment, or abuse of power. In fact, Dr. Summers had merely stated an idea that many scientists agree with. He suggested that innate differences between men and women may be one reason fewer women succeed in math and science careers. Dr. Summers was inviting further research and intellectual debate. However, he received a no-confidence vote from the Harvard faculty and was forced to resign.

Can you imagine what would have happened if Dr. Summers had suggested that men are the head of the home while women are to be submissive? I doubt he would have made it out of the room alive. In our culture the mere mention of different roles in marriage can set off a firestorm—even in our churches.

Submission is not a popular idea. It is not culturally acceptable or open for discussion in a society that worships equality. The idea of submission is never portrayed in our "the husband is an idiot married to a beautiful and brilliant woman" era of sitcoms. It's no surprise that God's roles in marriage are often so misunderstood and maligned. No wonder maintaining a submissive attitude can be so difficult.

BACK TO THE GARDEN

In the previous chapter, we peeked into the garden of Eden as God created the man and his wife. We read that God said it was not good for the man to be alone and created a helper for him. After God introduced these two, the Bible says, "The man and his wife were both naked, and they felt no shame" (Gen. 2:25).

Wow! A perfect man, a perfect woman, a perfect marriage. No sin, no selfishness . . . nothing to prevent this couple from being all God intended them to be. Sadly, this state of perfection did not last long. I'm sure you know the story. . . .

God planted a tree in the garden, calling it "the tree of the knowledge of good and evil" (Gen. 2:17), and told Adam not to eat from this tree. God gave this directive to Adam when he was alone, before the woman was created. We assume that Adam was to relate this message to his wife. The man was put in the position of being responsible for obedience to God's instruction.

THE CHOICE THAT CHANGED IT ALL

"Now the serpent was more crafty than any beast of the field . . ." Genesis 3:1 (NASB) describes. Have you ever considered why this wily serpent approached the woman instead of the man? I don't think it was because she *was* a woman, or that she was more easily fooled. I think the Serpent went to Eve because *she had not received the instructions directly from God.*

In other words, she was relying on Adam's leadership. Perhaps Adam had not clearly relayed God's message. We know Eve did not quote God's instructions verbatim. She added a few words. God had told Adam not to *eat* from the Tree of Knowledge of Good and Evil (Gen. 2:17). But when the Serpent questioned Eve, she told him, "God told us we can't eat from it *or touch it*" (see Gen. 3:3).

Perhaps the Serpent plucked the fruit off the branch and handed it to Eve. Nothing happened. She didn't die. Yet she was touching it. By adding to God's words, or misrepresenting them, she opened her mind to the possibility that God was wrong. All that the Serpent needed was a little foothold, a little doubt, to question God's goodness.

Of course, hindsight is 20/20, but what if the woman had replied, "You know, let me check with Adam. God talked to him about that tree"?

Some commentators argue that Eve was deceived, therefore not entirely responsible for her actions. Maybe, but I find that hard to swallow (pun intended). Even if she didn't have all her facts straight, Eve knew that particular tree was prohibited. The woman chose to disobey God's Word. I like to remind my kids that every choice, good or bad, has a consequence. And in this case, it was a matter of life and death.

Immediately, Adam's and Eve's eyes were opened, and they realized they were naked and hid from God. How tragic! Their disobedience broke their bond of perfection. Shame, guilt, and embarrassment entered their relationship. But another result of Eve's choice related directly to her: "To the woman He said, 'I will greatly multiply your pain in childbirth, in pain you will bring forth children; yet your desire will be for your husband, and he will rule over you'" (Gen. 3:16 NASB).

Through that one choice, evil flooded the world and everything changed. Never again would life be free from the ravages of sin. Eve would experience pain in childbirth, and sorrow in raising children.

Adam and Eve also experienced heartbreaking loss in their marriage. God had created them to be a team. The man

Lessons from the Dance Floor

Years ago Michael surprised me with dancing lessons. As a little girl I was enchanted with musicals, especially those featuring Fred Astaire and Ginger Rogers. They danced with grace and elegance, and I just knew I had that same rhythm in me. So we joined ten other couples in an elementary school gym and began to learn the waltz, the fox-trot, and even the tango.

Our dancing was not even remotely similar to what I'd seen on television. However, as we learned the steps, we also saw a correlation to our roles in marriage.

First, we learned that if I didn't follow Michael's lead, we just stood there. Because I spent most of the time going backward, following his lead was an act of faith. More importantly, I had to "feel" Michael's lead to be able to dance. Sometimes I needed Michael to direct more clearly, which meant he needed to place more pressure on my back or hand.

It's the same in our marriages. Sometimes wives can't follow because we don't know where our husband is going. We need to ask our husbands to be clear as they lead so we can dance!

was the perfect head and his wife the perfect helpmeet. But now that was irreparably broken.

Much has been made of the word "desire" in Genesis 3:16. Often, the word is given a sexual connotation, as in "you will lust after your husband, or desire him sexually." But in this context that doesn't make much sense. What would sexual desire for her husband have to do with him ruling over her? How could that be a part of God's judgment? In most marriages, a sexually enthusiastic wife would be helpful to the relationship, rather than detrimental. (And all the men said, "AMEN").

That same word, "desire," appears in a completely different circumstance in the story of Cain and Abel. In Genesis 4 we learn that Cain and Abel brought sacrifices to the Lord. But God rejected Cain's sacrifice, and Cain reacted with rage!

Then the Lord said to Cain, "Why are you angry? And why has your countenance fallen? If you do well, will not your countenance be lifted up? And if you do not do well, sin is crouching at the door; and its desire is for you, but you must master it" (Gen. 4:6–7 NASB).

Obviously, sin does not desire Cain sexually. Rather, the desire is for control. If Cain could not master his anger, sin would control him. The word "desire" is the same in both contexts. It makes much more sense for Eve to desire to control her husband, while finding that instead, he will rule over her.

Let me make one very important point. God's judgment does not authorize man to be an abusive, authoritarian despot.

Instead, in this Scripture God was reinstating the head/helper roles that He gave to the man and woman in Paradise. However, with the emergence of sin, these roles became a point of tension rather than a result of the teammate relationship that God intended.

No Hide-and-Seek?

I am a visual learner. When I read a story I see it in my mind, like a movie or a snapshot. For years I envisioned Eve and the Serpent talking, with Adam in the distance somewhere tending the garden or frolicking with the animals. But Genesis 3:6 says Adam was "with" Eve. It doesn't appear that Eve had to go find Adam. If he wasn't standing right beside her, he could have been within earshot . . . perhaps listening to the debate between the Serpent and Eve. If this was the case, Adam was abdicating his role of leadership. Eve picked it up. She ate and gave the fruit to him. She led. Now God was telling Eve to put the mantle of leadership back down . . . and forcing Adam to pick it back up.

EVE AND MARY

Eve had it all. She lived in a beautiful garden, had an abundance of food and a godly man, and never had to worry about what she wore. Life could not have been more perfect. But Eve believed the lie that God was withholding something better. She craved power and control. She wanted to be like God.

Eve had all the information she needed to make a wise choice. Although she may have had limited comprehension of God's ways, she did know God's character. God had forbidden the couple to eat the fruit from that one tree. That should have been all Eve needed to know. Rather than relying on her understanding of God's character, she decided to choose for herself.

Eve's decision ended all that was good. She lost her home, her happy relationship, and the easy life she enjoyed. One disobedient choice had devastating results. But the choice was all hers. No one made her take the fruit and place it to her lips. No one forced her. She doubted God's love and chose her own fate. If Eve had chosen to obey God's command, she would have remained in that ideal environment.

I think we are all like Eve. Every day, whether we fully grasp it or not, we face a choice whether or not to follow God's will. But we can't base our decision on our own limited understanding. We must base it on the truth of who God is.

Sometimes God requires things that don't make sense to our finite minds. We may attempt to mold God's instructions to fit our comfort zone. But God can see what we cannot, and knows far more than we can ever appreciate. Just like Eve in the garden, we may not agree with some directions God gives. But God realizes the implications of our obedience or disobedience even when we don't. And His plans are always for our ultimate best (Jeremiah 29:11).

Eve was not the only woman in Scripture who faced a dilemma of faith. Another young woman also encountered the challenge of obeying God's will. Although her life was certainly not perfect, it was going quite well for a Jewish girl. She lived in Nazareth and was engaged to a wonderful man. But all that would end when Mary chose to obey God's design for her life. The angel Gabriel appeared to Mary . . .

The angel went to her and said, "Greetings, you who are highly favored! The Lord is with you." Mary was greatly troubled at his words and wondered what kind of greeting this might be. But the angel said to her, "Do not be afraid, Mary, you have found favor with God. You will be with child and give birth to a son, and you are to give him the name Jesus" (Luke 1:28–31).

Mary was favored by God. He chose to pour His grace on her. This statement troubled her because she did not see herself as special. She was a normal Jewish girl, yet she gained God's notice. The angel tried to prepare Mary for his next few words by starting with, "Don't be afraid." But she wasn't afraid, not yet. She was perplexed.

"You will be with child and give birth to a son. . . ." Ah, now the reason for fear. Mary, the young girl favored by God, had a problem. She wasn't married, and she was a virgin. When Joseph found out about Mary's pregnancy, he would have every right to divorce her, which would bring disgrace upon Mary and her family. An unmarried woman with a child would never find a husband, leaving her without any means of support when her parents died.

Even more drastic was the rule of Hebrew law, which stated that a woman caught in infidelity should be stoned. Although that was not the common practice during Mary's day, it was still a potential threat. Mary had every reason to be afraid, yet she was not.

After clearing up her questions with the angel concerning her virginal conception, Mary responded with eagerness to serve her God:

"I am the Lord's servant," Mary answered. "May it be to me as you have said" (Luke 1:38).

Though young, Mary was not ignorant. She knew the God of the Old Testament (Luke 1:46–55), and was ready to follow His path. Mary was sure of her relationship to her God. She was His humble servant and felt privileged to obey Him, even though it was inconvenient and she would be misunderstood.

Table Talk

I must admit that I occasionally feel uncomfortable when I speak to groups of women about submission. I know some women think I sound antiquated at best and ignorant at worst.

My husband and I were having dinner with acquaintances recently when someone asked about the topic of the book I was writing. Although I am not ashamed about my subject, I do know it is often misunderstood. So I usually make a joke like, "You really don't want to know." But they do, so I tell them. "I'm writing on how to respect your husband through submission."

When I said this, one of our female dinner companions was visibly angry. Her face grew red and her voice shook as she told me her pastor said, "We don't have to obey our husbands."

I assured her that my understanding of submission was not that simple, and that I had no intention of trying to persuade her to my point of view. I was surprised at her reaction, because I knew her husband was a kind and gentle man.

As we continued to interact, I discovered that her husband had once, many years earlier, asked her to help him in a way that she felt was beneath her dignity. His request was not out of line, but she still did not want any part of it. She ultimately did as he asked, but she had always resented him for it. From then on she determined to never do anything she didn't want to do.

Again, her attitude was surprising. This was a woman who talked often and loudly about her love and obedience to Christ. Yet she could not see any correlation between her service to Christ and her service to her husband.

Mary's response to the angel's proclamation was remarkable: "May it be to me as you have said."

Mary's pregnancy would throw her ordinary life into immediate ruin. She had no idea how Joseph or her parents would respond, or if they would even believe her. She could certainly expect the judgment and ridicule of her hometown. Mary knew she would be misunderstood. Yet she chose to trust God anyway.

WHAT ABOUT THE MAN?

The need to control our husbands began in the garden, and we still struggle with it. The one constant I found in interviewing women for this book was the difficulty in giving up control. Like Eve, we want to make the choices that determine our lives.

A myriad of factors can thwart our desire to cooperate with God and our husbands. The remaining chapters of this book will explore some of these situations. We will look at submission in circumstances of sin, unbelief, poor health, and cultural factors. You may not find yourself in a marriage exactly like the ones you'll read about; however, I'm confident you will learn principles from these godly women that are applicable to any marriage.

Let me share several discoveries I made during my interviews. The women in these chapters are some of the most resourceful, courageous, and determined people I know. The stereotype of a submissive woman is that she is weak, silent, and even downtrodden. I didn't speak with one woman who would fit this stereotype. Every one had great strength of mind and spirit. They were good thinkers, hard workers, and willing partners who chose to trust God even when it was tough.

I've concluded that an act of submission means the most when a woman is strong and confident in her own right. Most husbands understand what it means for their strong-minded wives to follow their leads. Men appreciate this as the ultimate sign of respect.

Additionally, these women took on the role of helpmate *regardless of their husbands' actions*. They chose to honor God by subscribing to the precepts of His Word. None of these women chose submission because they were told to, but because they wanted to. They took deliberate steps to follow their husband's leadership in good and bad circumstances.

Finally, I found that the head/helper relationship is not a carbon copy in each home. Like a private dance, each couple fleshed out their complementarian roles to fit their personal situation.

I'm Third

For several summers my children attended a sports camp in Pennsylvania. This camp was perfect for my athletic children. They learned, among other things, that a competitive spirit was perfectly acceptable during sporting events. However, that spirit was discouraged off the field. In fact, the camp had a motto that was drilled into my children's brains: God first, others second, I'm third. In short, they were taught to remember,

"I'm third." This was not what I expected in the "We're #1" sports world. However, I was delighted by it. I even saw it in action in their attitudes and behavior in their first few weeks home from camp.

This maxim is not the norm in our culture. It reminds me of what happened in the 1976 Special Olympics, held in Spokane, Washington. Nine contestants, all physically or mentally disabled, assembled at the starting line for a track-and-field event. At the gun, they all started out, not exactly in a dash, but with a relish to run the race to the finish, and win.

Then one boy stumbled on the asphalt, tumbled, and began to cry. A few of the other athletes stopped their race to go check on their fallen comrade. Then those contestants linked arms and helped the boy get to the finish line together.

This is what Christ calls us to. We need to learn to come alongside our husbands in a way that allows us all to win. I'd rather cross life's finish line third than be first and all alone.

Without a Word

Submission and the Nonbelieving Husband

Wives, in the same way be submissive to your husbands so that, if any of them do not believe the word, they may be won over without words by the behavior of their wives, when they see the purity and reverence of your lives.

—*1 Peter 3:1–2*

SUSAN BEGAN DATING John while they were just sophomores in high school. Although she had gone out with other boys once or twice, John was her first and only boyfriend. They dated six years and nineteen days, marrying after college graduation.

During their courtship Susan and John never talked about God. Both were raised to go to church, at least occasionally, and Susan assumed they would do so after the wedding. John even said he would go with her, but it never really happened. At that time, all Susan wanted was to be seen in church with John, sitting by her in the pew. She felt that would make her look better to others. It was something you were supposed to do, just like her parents had done. But as John found reasons not to attend church each week, Susan also began to stay home.

After several years of marriage and three sons, Susan returned to church so her children would be raised in Sunday school. Although John had promised to attend church after the children were born, he still did not do so. In fact, for the forty years they have been married, John has yet to show any interest in spiritual things.

AN ENCOUNTER WITH CHRIST

John and Susan had been married ten years when Susan was invited to attend a community Bible study. For the first time in her life, Susan studied God's Word verse by verse and quickly began to grow spiritually. As Susan's faith developed, John seemed to sense a threat, and the spiritual barrier between them grew wider.

At first, Susan tried to share what she was learning, or quoted biblical principles in their discussions. These attempts to help John "see the light" only caused greater distance. He considered her desire for righteousness to be judgmental piety. The more she tried to witness to John, the more he resisted.

Susan observed her friends who were married to men who shared a common bond in Christ and longed for that kind of relationship with John. She fantasized about being married to someone who would pray with her, lead the family in devotions, or even attend church. Susan prayed fervently for a change in her husband and used every opportunity to guide John toward Christ. Nothing seemed to change their situation. Nothing seemed to change John.

STARTLING REVELATIONS

She's not sure when it happened, but Susan came to some startling revelations. As she prayed for John, she realized that she was going about her witness all the wrong way. She realized that John was exactly the man she had married. He had the same strengths he had possessed on their wedding day. He still loved her. He was a generous provider. He was a kind man. John had not grown into a different person; she had. Yes, her encounter with Christ brought her spiritual life, but it appeared to be destroying her marriage. Susan was certain that this was not what Christ would want.

Susan realized the spiritual expectations she now had for John were unfair. She realized she needed to accept John for who he was, not for who she wanted him to be.

As Susan began to recognize John's free will, her eyes were opened to the damage she was doing by trying to manipulate John with her "gentle words," rather than letting God deal with John on His own terms. She had forgotten that John did not have the resources to appraise spiritual things. He wasn't rejecting her or belittling what was important to her. John simply did not have the spiritual economy to respond to her overtures.

Susan discovered that her attitude toward John was not respectful. She saw herself as spiritually superior. Susan remembered that Romans 5:8 tells us that Christ died for us while we were still sinners. She realized that God valued John just as much as He valued her. God longed for John to come to a saving faith more than Susan longed for that, and her attitude only hindered the process.

Susan thought she was following the biblical admonition to win her husband for Christ without a word and with a gentle and quiet spirit (1 Peter 3:1–2). However, she became conscious of how her behavior conflicted with her silence. When she left for church with the kids in tow, she often sighed or huffed as she closed the door, glaring at John as he sat happily reading the Sunday sports section. She made a production of studying her Bible, with notes and commentaries spread all over the dining room table, hoping John would be impressed with her knowledge. Susan sprinkled her speech with "the Bible says ..." or "God told me ..." or even "Praise the Lord," which left John confused and frustrated. She even got on her knees at night before she climbed into bed, thinking her posture would somehow woo John to Christ. Although she had quit pleading with John to attend church, Susan was anything but silent.

UNDERSTANDING SUBMISSION

Sensing God's leading, Susan decided to make some changes in her approach. She studied everything the Bible said about being a wife, and chose to apply these principles to her life. First, she asked John's forgiveness for her attitude. She explained that she wanted John to believe in Christ, but that she was sorry for making him feel uncomfortable or guilty about his choices. Then she asked John's permission to continue attending church and leading a small group in her community Bible study.

From experience, Susan knew John often saw her Bible study leadership as a nuisance. Because of leadership preparation and attending leaders' meetings, she was not available to spend much time with John in the evenings. As she expected, John happily gave his consent for her to continue attending church, and he even encouraged her to continue taking the kids.

However, although he did not mind her attending the Bible study, he asked her to give up her leadership role at the end of the year. Susan was surprised by her own reaction. She felt total peace for the first time in years, knowing that she was free from the need to control John's spiritual life, and was giving him the respect he was due as the God-ordained leader of their home.

Susan's behavior also changed. She kissed John on the way

out the door for church, knowing he would look forward to her return. She no longer made a production of her Bible study, but put it away when John approached so she would not be tempted to play the Holy Spirit in his life. She quit telling John what the Bible said. Instead she brought biblical principles into their discussions without referencing the passage or pointing out that God had said it first.

Susan did not focus on the outward appearances of spirituality at all. She decided to focus on being the best wife and helpmate possible, understanding that this was what the apostle Peter meant when he encouraged wives to win their unbelieving husbands without a word. Susan knew her loving actions—and not the noise she'd been spewing from her mouth—would be the Holy Spirit's megaphone.

MOURNING YOUR LOSS

As young girls we may have dreamed about Prince Charming coming to sweep us off our feet. As we grew older, we usually realized that our expectations weren't realistic. There are no perfect husbands, just as there are no perfect wives. Yet we still long for what we do not have in our lives and in our relationships. We often fall in the "if only" trap. "If only he would . . ." We assume that if our husbands would change their beliefs or behavior, our lives would be more satisfying.

When we are in Susan's situation, it's important to grieve the loss of the dream.

You may long for a husband who loves Christ as you want him to, but that might not be your reality. Unfortunately, when our head is full of wishes, we might miss what God has in store for us right where we are. We will never be able to see God's goodness in our current circumstances if we focus on our mates' negative qualities. We won't be able to appreciate our husbands as God's gift to us if we hold on to an unrealistic or unfair expectation of who he should be.

Mourning the dream will give you the ability to discern God's work around you. Just because God has not said yes to your righteous prayer that doesn't mean He has forgotten you. God may be working in you or through you in an unexpected way. Susan is a prime example of a woman grieving over her loss and moving on. Yes, we still need to pray for our husbands, but adjusting our hopes will allow us to accept them, and respect them accordingly.

Elisabeth Kubler-Ross identified five stages of grief in her 1969 book, *On Death and Dying*.[1] Although these stages were originally recognized in respect to death, they may be applied to any loss. The stages include:

1. Denial: *"If I can only get my husband to church, he'll believe."*
2. Anger: either aimed at the unbelieving spouse or God
3. Bargaining: *"God, if you'll change my husband, I'll _____."*

4. Depression: *"Why read my Bible? God doesn't care!"*
5. Acceptance: *"God, You have Your plan. I'll choose to trust You."*

Any of the first four stages will rob you of the freedom to respect your husband as God desires. When you can finally accept your situation, you will be able to love and respect your husband in a way that will bring honor to God.

STILL CHANGING AFTER ALL THESE YEARS

Even after being married for more than forty years, Susan is still learning how to be a godly wife. One evening a few years ago, John and Susan were in the kitchen making dinner. While she cooked over the stove, John started to make a salad. As she placed dinner on the table, Susan noticed that John had made a salad for himself, but had not made one for her. Surprised by this, she asked him why. He said, "Because no matter how I make it, you'd gripe."

This stopped Susan in her tracks.

"Do I do that? Do I complain about everything?" she asked.

"Everything," John replied.

Susan had no idea that she was this way. Once again, God used her unbelieving husband to mold her into His image. As she looked back, Susan knew that John was right. Susan had studied the book of Philippians and was well acquainted with the verses: "Do all things without grumbling or disputing; so that you will prove yourselves to be blameless and innocent, children of God above reproach in the midst of a crooked and perverse generation, among whom you appear as lights in the world" (Phil. 2:14–15 NASB). Susan was in jeopardy of hiding the light within her due to an ungrateful spirit.

Becoming aware of this flaw, Susan set out to change her attitude again. She marveled at how this revolutionized her marriage. She no longer complained or nagged to get John to do something. Susan would mention to John what she wanted done, perhaps a garden planted, but left it there. After time passed, she found that John did things for her willingly—not because of her constant complaints but because he chose to do things that would make her happy.

Susan began to understand that by approaching John with an attitude of submission, she was lining herself up under God's authority. She saw God lead their family time and again through the decisions of her unbelieving husband. She was also amazed to see God use even John's poor decisions to work in his life, as long as she stepped out of God's way and didn't gripe about the results.

The Truth about Nagging

Several years ago I bought my husband a portable GPS system for his car. We found it was a great help when we were lost, or didn't have any idea where we were going. But we also found that, at times, the GPS gave us a route to our destination that was worse than the one we usually drove. We were amused to find that when we disobeyed the GPS directions, the female computerized voice would give us guidance over and over, attempting to get us back on her route. We dubbed her the "nagivator." When the GPS became particularly annoying, one of us would reach over and turn her off. The silence was golden!

Unfortunately, it is all too easy for the wife to become the nagivator in our husbands' lives. We want things to be done a certain way, or in a specific time frame. When our husbands don't follow our desires, we say the same thing over and over again.

When they do complete a task we've requested, we might even complain that it wasn't done the "right" way. We encountered this problem with loading the dishwasher. For years Michael would load, and I would rearrange.

"Why help her, she won't like how I did it anyway," he decided. It took awhile for me to realize that I was my own worst enemy. I wanted help around the house, but judged Michael's attempts to support me as not quite good enough.

Changing my strategy, I've learned to appreciate any assistance I receive. I say a sincere thanks and don't criticize the results. I've had to ask myself, "Which is more important, the task or the man?"

I've also discovered that evenings are not the best time to request Michael's help with home repair. However, if we set aside a Saturday morning, we both have the energy to tackle a project with minimal fuss. This also frees me from the desire to pester him, knowing the project will be attended to in due time.

Being the nagivator in our home will not bring a satisfactory outcome. Our husbands will discover that it is much easier to simply tune us out or turn us off. As Proverbs 19:13 (NASB) puts it, "The contentions of a wife are a constant dripping." Like a leaky faucet that breaks the quiet of a still night, a wife's complaining becomes an annoying disruption to the prospect of a peaceful home.

THE FINAL ANSWER IS . . .

The verdict is still out. John has not yet professed faith in Jesus Christ. Otherwise, they have a good marriage. Susan loves John unconditionally as the man God chose for her to partner with for life. She enjoys spending time with him. She prays for John every day, and follows Scripture in her role as a wife married to a nonbeliever. Susan had to grieve over the loss of her dream to share a faith with her husband. Susan had to learn to relinquish her desire to control John's spiritual journey.

In all this Susan is sure of one thing. All her words, her disappointment in John's lack of spiritual interest, and her repeated attempts to be the Holy Spirit in his life will never bring John to faith. In fact, she's fairly sure the path she was on would have been toxic to both his faith and their marriage if she had not learned to give God control of John's eternal future.

Susan observes that often Christian wives are so "super-spiritual" that they inadvertently push their husbands away from the very thing they desire most. With their words or manipulative actions, they forever extinguish spiritual dialogue with their husbands. Susan wonders how many husbands would consider Christ if they didn't fear their wives would treat this conversion as a personal victory rather than the work of the Holy Spirit.

BUILDING HIS REPUTATION

A good woman is hard to find, and worth far more than diamonds. . . . Her husband is greatly respected when he deliberates with the city fathers (Prov. 31:10, 23 THE MESSAGE).

One of the greatest gifts we can give to our husbands is to bring them honor and respect outside of our home. A wife must carefully consider how she represents her unbelieving husband among her believing friends. To somehow denigrate his leadership by comparing him to other men or complaining about his lack of spirituality can damage his reputation.

Of course, we want to ask our praying friends to take our husband's eternal destiny before our heavenly Father, but a constant lament won't further Christ's cause in your home. Should your husband meet someone from your church or Bible study, you want them to feel they can approach your husband with genuine respect, not with suspicion or pity because he has not come to faith in Jesus Christ.

As wives, we have great power over our husband's public persona. Our goal must be to honor our husbands in such a way that they are respected in our community.

Encouraging His Spiritual Leadership

Women have often complained to me about their husband's lack of spiritual leadership. Because my husband was the senior pastor in our church, they assumed that he and I spent most of our waking hours in spiritual conversation, or that we studied the Bible together for hours at a time.

Neither of these scenarios was true. We both prefer to study our Bibles individually. Certainly reading God's Word together does provide intimacy, but it just doesn't work for us.

However, we will talk about what we are learning. Not every day, perhaps not even weekly. Sometimes I'll read a passage to Michael that is meaningful to me, and tell him how I am applying it to my life. He will do the same with me. This is never a planned time of sharing, but rather a spontaneous conversation as we ponder a problem or a new insight.

Nor do we spend hours praying together. We do pray most nights before we fall asleep. We also pray before big decisions or when one of us has a burden. But, again, this is not a time specifically set aside for prayer, other than at bedtime.

I think it is important that women know what the spiritual life looks like in other families. We set our hopes high, and then complain when our expectations are not met. Usually our expectations are false. We make assumptions about what other couples do; some-times we even exaggerate our own habits for fear of not looking spiritual to our church friends.

But, wives, we can encourage our husband's spiri-tual leadership. Here are a few simple suggestions:

1. Approach your husband with something specific to pray about. Speak thoughtfully, not threaten-ingly. Say things like, "Honey, would you pray for me right now? I'm really concerned about _____ and would so appreciate having you pray for me." Refrain from saying, "We need to pray about this." Approach your husband with your need, not his.

2. Share your personal insights into Scripture with your husband—but not with the agenda of

changing him. Begin with, "I read the coolest thing today—can I read it to you?" Then explain how you apply it to your <u>own</u> life.

3. Begin a family question each night at dinner. Occasionally, perhaps once a week, ask "What is God teaching you right now?"

4. Don't demean your husband for not meeting your expectations. Never demand that he grow spiritually. Ultimately, that is between your husband and God.

NOTE
1. Elisabeth Kübler-Ross, *On Death and Dying,* (New York: Macmillan, 1969).

The Caregiver

Submission to a Husband with a Chronic Illness

Bear one another's burdens, and thereby
fulfill the law of Christ.

—*Galatians 6:2 NASB*

"I, CINDY, TAKE YOU, Michael, to be my wedded husband, to have and to hold from this day forward, for better, for worse, for richer, for poorer, in sickness or in health, to love and to cherish, until death do us part, according to God's holy ordinance; thereto I pledge my love."

Maybe you recited words like these at your wedding. You certainly meant them. But your naïve mind probably only saw endless possibilities of goodness for your future.

When you spoke these words at your minister's prompting, you probably heard them more like this: "I take you to be my husband for BETTER, for worse, for RICHER, for poorer, in sickness or in HEALTH, to LOVE and CHERISH. . . ."

Most of us would never have considered the "other" words that could become predominate in our married lives: worse . . . poorer . . . sickness.

REAL WOMEN, REAL HELPMATES

On a warm July morning, in the Washington D.C. suburbs, I spoke with two women who had experienced these "other" words to a depth that most of us can't even imagine. These are women whom I know. Women whose lives I have witnessed, whose marriages have stood firm in the worst of times. These women took the role of helpmeet to a new level as each of their husbands battled sickness that could have been "until death do us part."

Gwen had been married for five years and was pregnant with their first child when her husband was diagnosed with a rare liver disease. Until that point in their lives, Gwen had always been well cared for. Jim loved her immensely and provided her every need. For the next ten years Jim battled the disease with little success.

By this time Jim and Gwen had two young children, and it became apparent that the only viable solution for Jim would be a liver transplant. Almost immediately Jim's body began rejecting his new liver. He spent most of the next eight months in a hospital more than an hour away from their home, often on the brink of death. Eventually Jim was able to return to work, but during the next six years, he spent nearly two years hospitalized, recuperating at home, dealing with complications of surgery, or facing other issues related to his transplant.

Mel is a soldier's wife. She first spotted Brian in her brother-in-law's military yearbook. In 2001 Brian was a Lt. Colonel in the United States Army. Brian had served our country in South Korea, Germany, and in the Gulf War, but now was positioned in the relative safety of the Pentagon.

On September 11, 2001, Brian had just stepped away from his office when American Airlines Flight 77 crashed into the Pentagon. If Brian had been at his desk, he would have died instantly. Instead, he was caught in the aftermath of the explosion, which left 60 percent of his body covered with burns. More than 20 percent of his body was covered with third-degree burns.

Brian endured more than thirty surgeries, and the unimaginable pain of living through the burn recovery process.[1]

As the summer sun streamed through the windows, I sat with these women and asked them about their marriages. They had each been placed into the role of caregiver, not just helping with the normal needs of a husband but going far beyond that, becoming the nurse, chauffer, accountant, and medical liaison, often denying their own desires and their children's needs when their husbands' survival superseded all else.

I wondered how the reversal in their marriage roles had

affected their views of being a helper. What did submission look like when your husband could not physically, mentally, or emotionally lead your home?

LEARNING TO PROTECT HIS MANHOOD

Both Gwen and Mel were thrown into immediate situations in which they needed to make all the decisions. This included all the normal events in the family, as well as all their husbands' medical decisions. Mel told me that Brian's injuries were so incapacitating that he could not even sign a power of attorney. These women had no choice but to take control, even fighting to get the necessary medical attention their husbands so desperately needed.

During this time Gwen and Mel learned the meaning of true submission. It wasn't in the control, it wasn't in the decision-making process, it was in their attitude that reflected to their husbands, "You are still a man."

Men have an innate need for respect. In *For Women Only,* Shaunti Feldhahn writes, "The male need for respect . . . is so hardwired and critical that most men would rather feel unloved than disrespected or inadequate."[2]

This need did not magically disappear when Jim and Brian were ill. It was probably even more prevalent because they could not participate in the leadership of their homes. Their wives needed them and their children needed them, but they weren't in a position to offer any guidance. Jim and Brian were not only physically incapacitated, but they were also stripped of their very essence of manhood. They were not just battling health problems, but also an identity crisis. Fortunately for these men, their wives were sensitive to this need. Gwen and Mel each determined to do everything in their power to protect their husbands' manhood.

For Mel, that meant including Brian in every decision. The goal was to get Brian healthy. Mel realized that for Brian to own that goal, he needed to have a voice in how to achieve it. Often his thoughts were jumbled because of his heavy pain medication; however, Mel knew that Brian needed to be respected as leader. So she took the time to discuss each decision with him, even when it would have been easier or more expedient to make decisions without his input.

Mel often reminded Brian, "This is exactly where God wants us to be right now." Brian was able to sense that Mel was still willing to follow his lead. She did not think he was inadequate or worth less as her husband than he had been on September 10, 2001.

The Household Administrator

When Michael and I were first married, we assumed that he would pay the bills, balance the checkbook, handle our insurance, prepare our taxes, and so forth.

That's how our folks had done it and we never considered challenging that system.

After a couple of years of marriage, Michael was increasingly tired of doing those things. At the same time I was employed in the banking industry. One day it dawned on us that I was better equipped to do those things. I actually enjoyed balancing the checkbook and doing our taxes. I felt a victory each time I found a few extra dollars. We realized that the financial tasks of our household were not an obligation of leadership but rather an assignment of administration. Since then I have managed all of our accounts, from the checkbook to investments, with Michael's agreement and gratitude.

If your spouse is the administrator of your home, you still need to understand the basics of your financial situation. You should have a working knowledge of your bank accounts, bills, and investments so you are ready to step into that role if it is necessary.

I encourage you to have a written document that explains all of your financial information, including account numbers and access codes, in safekeeping should the need arise for someone else to take over.

Gwen noticed a change in Jim, especially as it related to their children. During Jim's lengthy hospitalizations, Gwen often took on the role of father as well as mother. As Jim was less involved with the kids, he began to withdraw.

Wisely, Gwen chose to purposefully involve Jim in the leadership of their family life. Before his transplant, Jim had been working with their young son on personal hygiene. As weeks passed without Dad at home, these hygiene practices began to go by the wayside. Gwen had reminded, cajoled, and threatened to no avail. Then she realized her children needed to feel the presence of their father in the home, as much as Jim needed to remain leader of the home. So, the next time this issue came up, Gwen looked at her son and said, "I'm going to the hospital to visit your dad. When I do, I will tell him about your disobedience." With a look of horror, her son ran upstairs to brush his teeth. True to her word, later that morning, Gwen related this incident to Jim.

"You should have seen the look of pleasure in Jim's eyes," she recalled. "He knew he still had a place in our home, even though he was absent."

Gwen learned that she had to carefully represent their father to her children. Jim was still their father, even with diminished capacity. "How I talk to them about Jim affects their view of him."

After that moment Gwen often told her children, "I'll ask Daddy about that." Gwen showed her respect for Jim's leadership by protecting his manhood.

Lesson from a Pressure Cooker

When I was a child, my mother canned fruits and vegetables. I vividly remember her preparing the Ball canning jars and placing them in our pressure cooker. Before fastening the lid over the cooker she would shoo her kids out of the kitchen with the warning, "stand back in case it blows." If my mother did not let enough steam escape through the pressure release valve, there was a slight danger that the lid could blow right off.

Our husbands are like pressure cookers, and we have the ability to help them either release steam or explode. Poor health is only one issue that can add pressure to our marriage. Our husbands often live under the weight of unrealized goals. They may hate their job, feel themselves to be inadequate providers, or experience stress related to the high expectations of their employer, or. . . their wife. Sometimes we forget the burdens our spouses carry on a daily basis.

Our husbands may have pressure building in them. It will eventually manifest itself, either externally in the form of anger and depression, or internally in the form of illness or heart failure. As their wife, we usually know what would help them release that pressure, and what will send them to the brink of explosion.

Watch for signs of built up pressure in your husband. Encourage him to make healthy adjustments that would allow him to safely release his pent up frustration. While women may shop, or spend time with friends in an effort to reduce stress, men may benefit from physical exercise, or a hands-on project. Others may experience relief through a hobby, or simply spending time alone.

Encourage your husband verbally. Appreciate the stress he carries and support his efforts with your respect and confidence.

THE CONTROL FREAK REFORMATION PROGRAM

The next step in Gwen's and Mel's journies came when their husbands were healing, returning to work, and ready to assume the mantle of leadership in the home.

Mel called it her control freak reformation program. She realized that she was exhausted from feeling like she was doing everything. But Brian was willing, and increasingly able, to do what he could. Mel recognized that she was hording power. She had become accustomed to helping Brian with every area of his life. He needed help in the shower, in the bathroom, even getting out of a chair. Additionally, Brian was having problems with short-term memory, so Mel caught herself constantly reminding him.

Mel realized that her need for control was scarring her relationship with Brian, who felt disrespected and resentful. In hording control, Mel was keeping Brian from fulfilling the role of leadership God had designed him for. There was no benefit for Mel to have a discouraged husband.

Gwen had a similar experience when Jim was ready to step back into his leadership role. After spending months learning how to run their home, Gwen found she was quite efficient. She started telling Jim "how things were done now."

Of course, Jim would have gladly listened to Gwen's opinions, but Gwen understood that she was demoralizing her husband by talking that way. "I'm taking the life out of Jim by taking his role in our family," she realized.

FOR BETTER OR WORSE

As we finished our coffee that morning, I asked my friends what advice they would give to a woman facing the extreme circumstances that they had been through. What would they say to a woman who was about to face the "other" words in her vows?

1. Keep in mind that marriage is a marathon, not a sprint. Take time to adjust to your new situation. Gwen and Mel agreed that you never "return to normal," rather you have a new normal.
2. Don't give up! Don't blame God. This doesn't mean you can't question or get angry at your circumstances—just don't stay there. Sometimes you have to tell yourself, "I will not give up."
3. Be secure in who you are and in the Lord. Only then can you understand God's roles in marriage. It's about give-and-take. Your husband is the leader and you are his teammate, his helper. Mel and Brian have given their lives to supporting families recovering from burn injuries. Mel has seen far too many wives walk away because they don't know who they are. It's never too late to change.
4. Finally, remember you made a covenant with your husband, and with God. It's not about you.

One day, as Gwen cleaned the wound in Jim's side, he said, "This is more than you signed up for."

"No Jim, this is exactly what I signed up for. I just never thought it would happen."

Are You a Control Freak?

We've all had to deal with people who want to be in control of everyone and every situation. Controlling individuals can make life very uncomfortable for others. But have you ever stopped to consider if you might be the control freak? Here are a few questions to ask yourself:

1. Do you have a "my way or the highway" attitude?
2. Do you have a hard time admitting mistakes?
3. Will you yell to get your way and sulk when you don't?
4. Are you a perfectionist? Do you berate yourself when you make a mistake?
5. Are you able to delegate to your husband and children?
6. Does your family tease you about being bossy?

7. Do you feel the need to comment on everyone's behavior, relationships, or even the clothes they wear?

Without meaning to, controlling individuals send hurtful messages to others. They may make harmful remarks, and imply that their husbands and children are inadequate or incapable. If you believe this describes you, get help to regain your balance.

Talk with your family. Admit your need to control and ask for their help. Set appropriate boundaries in what you will ask of them, and have a prearranged word or phrase they can use to alert you before you step over the line.

Delegate. Give them some of your tasks and allow them freedom to complete the job without your supervision or criticism.

Remember that life is not a competition. Give yourself freedom to fail.

NOTES
1. For Brian and Mel Birdwell's entire story read *Refined by Fire* (Wheaton: Tyndale House, 2004).
2. Shaunti Feldhahn, *For Men Only* (Sisters, OR: Multnomah, 2006), 22.

Codependency versus Submission

Is There a Difference?

Do not repay evil with evil or insult with insult, but with blessing, because to this you were called so that you may inherit a blessing.

—*1 Peter 3:9*

KATE AND WILL met at a campus ministry at the University of Wisconsin. He was the all-star athlete; she was the bright and beautiful coed. They had both been raised in conservative Christian homes, where alcohol was forbidden, along with most movies and dancing. They dated for two years and, much to the delight of their parents, were married in a wonderful celebration with a promise of happily ever after.

Both settled comfortably into married life and a dual income. They joined a church, found companionship in a close circle of friends, and enjoyed success in their careers. Over time, Will began to enjoy a beer or glass of wine occasionally, feeling the pressure to fit in socially with clients and business associates. Kate chose to join him, not wanting to appear prudish or judgmental. Although many people can consume alcohol without dependence, Will was not one of them. Within a short period of time, he began to drink to cover anxiety and disappointment, becoming a full-blown alcoholic.

During their early years of marriage, Kate discovered that Will had an explosive temper. She learned to preserve harmony in their home by always maintaining the status quo. Kate knew from experience that she would not get any satisfaction by confronting Will with his issues. So she chose to remain silent on the subject of drinking, as she had done with other conflicts that had arisen in their marriage.

As with most dysfunctional families, Kate and Will hid their problems from their circle of friends. Will rarely drank to excess in public. In fact, Kate was so good at keeping up their image that she continued to join Will in social drinking, monitoring his intake so she made sure they exited any party before Will had reached his limit.

Will and Kate kept up appearances at church. Kate worked in the children's ministry; Will helped set up Communion. No one knew about the heartache in their home. In fact, to most outsiders, Will and Kate had an ideal marriage. She appeared to be doting, he adoring—giving the impression that they were a model of the head/helper roles so often encouraged in their church.

In her own way, Kate *was* a helper to her husband. She

helped his alcoholism by being codependent. She played the role of the doormat wife, both in public and private, so Will felt the freedom to run his life without the checks and balances that a supportive wife should provide.

UNDERSTANDING CODEPENDENCY

Carol has dual credentials in the field of alcoholism and substance abuse. She is a clinical therapist, and also has personal experience as the wife of a recovering alcoholic. Like Kate, Carol was married to Gregg for several years before it was apparent that her husband had a dependency on alcohol. Carol had a classic codependent relationship with Gregg. It was much easier to ignore the problem, or make excuses for it, than do the hard work of intervention and recovery. To further complicate her thoughts, Carol equated submission with passivity.

Carol spoke with me candidly about life with an alcoholic. She told me of her years as a codependent to Gregg, when she blindly trusted him even to the point of watching their financial reserves dwindle away and debt rise without ever questioning him about the decisions he was making. When she did confront Gregg on his problem spending, he would react with anger. Carol would withdraw from the confrontation by responding in the role of a child, rather than remaining an adult and aggressively pursuing Gregg's accountability. Carol misunderstood her role of submission, feeling it was an excuse to avoid conflict and stay in denial.

Carol explained to me that women who are codependent to their husbands tend to feel powerless and take on the role of a victim. Typically, a woman like this responds in one of three ways:

1. She reacts passively to her husband's addiction to avoid conflict and keep the peace. She ignores the addiction, pretends that nothing is wrong, and works hard to hide the addictive behavior from friends and family, always maintaining the status quo. The goal of the passive wife is to avoid conflict at all costs, even if it means suppressing her own thoughts and feelings.

2. Some women react with passive/aggressive tendencies. In this case a woman may appear passive to avoid conflict, especially in reaction to her husband's addiction, but she may act out in other areas. For instance, she will be unwilling to confront her husband on the damage his addiction is doing to their relationship, but she may withhold sex as a punishment. She will deny anything is wrong, then blow up later for no apparent reason or give her husband the silent treatment. In doing this she is attempting to manipulate, or punish, her husband without ever explaining herself.

3. Women may also be codependent and act aggressively

toward their husbands. A woman may react to her husband's drunkenness with temper tantrums, throwing things, and screaming. She may use words that demean and shame, not expressing respect. Aggressiveness tends to provoke defensiveness from the addict rather than open communication and promote connectedness.

In all three of the cases, the women, as victims, still feel powerless to change the situation. They may react momentarily, but are too afraid or too immobilized to attempt to work with their husband to deal with the underlying issue of addiction.

Carol correlated codependency to a "parent-child" relationship. The wife takes on the role of the child, her husband the role of the parent. Like a child, a codependent wife expects to be taken care of without ever questioning her husband. When faced with her husband's addiction, she may respond childishly, with rebellion, tantrums, or pouting, rather than communicating her feelings in a mature, adult fashion. This relationship is lopsided, and nothing like the head/helper relationship that God intended.

REFRAMING SUBMISSION

Godly submission does not mean to let your husband choose sin or harmful habits without speaking up. We read that a gentle and quiet spirit is precious in God's sight (1 Peter 3:4) and worry that God expects a wife to *never* speak, *never* discuss problems, and *always* remain silent even in the face of sin in her home. But godly submission allows for good discussion.

I cannot be a helper to my husband, encouraging him to become the man God intends for him to be, without expressing my ideas, my thoughts, and my feelings. I won't fulfill my God-given role as helper to my husband without healthy communication. Submission is not a reluctance to speak but rather a respectful attitude *when* you speak. It is remembering that the role of leadership is a mantle placed on your husband by his Creator. We need to respect that role, even when we need to address a problem.

Godly submission means that we take our role as a helpmate to our husband seriously. Our job is to exercise our gifts as image-bearers of Christ to encourage our husband's godly leadership. When addictive behavior consumes a husband, whether it is a controlled substance, alcohol, or pornography, our place as helpmeet is to honestly and respectfully intervene in such a way that persuades him to seek the professional help he needs.

LEARNING HEALTHY COMMUNICATION

As a therapist, Carol teaches couples a technique of assertive communication with the acronym H.A.R.D. To a codependent wife, this form of communication may feel especially risky; however, it is one step in the direction of a healthy relationship.

The assertive approach is **honest**. It is straightforward without intent to manipulate or control. This requires that a woman identify her feelings, and think through how best to express them. The wife of an alcoholic may need to rehearse her words to a third party who will help her clarify her feelings and state them in a straightforward manner.

An assertive response needs to be given **appropriately**. This means you must choose the time, place, and atmosphere in which to communicate. It gives you the opportunity to choose a time when you are calm and in control of your own emotions. Even in a healthy relationship, appropriate timing is essential to good communication. For years I have lived by something I call the "three-day rule."

I discovered the idea for this rule while studying Esther 4:16. After deciding to approach the king (her husband) on behalf of the Jewish people, Esther took three days to fast and pray. I do not use my three days to fast, but I do pray over a significant issue, looking to God for help in approaching my husband in a way that will be respectful and beneficial to our relationship.

When I am upset with my husband, I give myself three days to cool off and determine my response before I confront him. The three days gives me time to think through the issue.

Sometimes after three days the issue has resolved itself. Often I realize I was overreacting, or being hormonally sensitive.

If after three days the issue still bothers me, I have had time to form my thoughts so that I know I am communicating in a way that gives me the best chance of being heard and understood.

Keeping a Bridled Tongue

I have the gift of sarcasm. OK, it's not a gift . . . especially not when I nail someone with a well-placed comment. Usually, sarcasm is meant to be humorous, but I discovered more often than not, my sarcasm expresses my true feelings of anger or bitterness. It's a way to communicate my dissatisfaction without facing the problem.

I've noticed when I am sarcastic toward my husband in public, I only make others around me uncomfortable. Clearly, there is a better and more appropriate way to express myself.

The Bible tells us to control our tongues because our speech will influence the rest of our behavior. A small bit in a horse's mouth can rein in the entire animal. In the same way our words can work either for us or against us. When we don't restrain our tongues, we can bring ourselves, and others, to ruin.

It's hard to speak kindly when we are wounded, or disappointed in someone we love. But the Bible encourages us to never pay back insult for insult, but to be a blessing instead (1 Peter 3:9).

Learning to communicate honestly and respectfully is one way to be a blessing to our husbands. I need to choose my words carefully and set my tone appropriately rather than rely on my quick wit to get my point across.

This is especially true when we are emotionally or physically injured. Our first impulse may be to insult our spouse, but like Proverbs 25:11 says, "A word aptly spoken is like apples of gold in settings of silver." Sarcasm is never a blessing.

Assertiveness must be **respectful**. We need to choose words that are gentle yet firm. We need to express our opinions without demeaning our husbands. Respectful communication is cultivated when we separate a husband's personhood from his addictive behavior. Remembering our husband's strengths and focusing on the love and value God places on him will help us communicate the grief and pain from the addiction, rather than attacking the husband personally.

Finally, assertive communication is **direct**. We must be clear and concise with our words. It is especially helpful if the wife of an addict can express herself unemotionally and state reasonable expectations of her husband.

People protect their addictions with a vengeance. Denial is a powerful form of deceit. Therefore, when a wife chooses to assertively confront her husband with his addiction, an intervention that includes other family, friends, pastors, or professional counselors would be advantageous. It's imperative that she has trusted individuals to tell of her struggles, people who will uphold her in prayer and offer wise feedback. She must let godly friends and family hold her accountable for her own motivations and behavior as a codependent to her husband's alcoholism.

UNCONDITIONAL LOVE

Carol herself grew from codependence to assertive communication. However, this was only one step in her own personal journey as the wife of an alcoholic. As a student of the Scriptures, Carol believed in her role as Gregg's helper and decided to do all she could, by God's power, to help Gregg confront his own issues. She realized that she had lost her love and respect for Gregg, and that scared her. She knew it was not God's will to live in a loveless marriage, and chose to make that one of her first priorities.

One evening Carol decided to wait on the front steps of their home for Gregg to return from work. She gently expressed her lack of feelings and her fear, acknowledging that Gregg's alcoholism was interfering in their relationship. Her calm honesty shocked Gregg enough that he chose to give up drinking.

Eventually, Gregg returned to his addiction. However, those few months gave Carol the time she needed to remember who Gregg was without alcohol, and to plead with God to love him through her. When Gregg did start drinking alcohol again, God had worked in Carol so that she regained her love and respect for Gregg as a person and could separate that from his addictive behavior. This gave Carol the freedom to detach herself emotionally in a way that allowed her to take steps that were not self-serving, but truly in her husband's best interest.

For motivation to overcome any addiction (drugs, alcohol, pornography), the addict must experience a consequence that is greater than the addiction. Knowing this, Carol chose to move out of the bedroom she shared with Gregg, into another room in their home. She explained to Gregg that she still loved him but could no longer support his choices. She would honestly tell him, "I long for us to be back together. I feel so sad because I don't know what it will take. I miss you."[1]

Carol began attending Al-Anon meetings for families of alcoholics and signed up for therapy with a Christian counselor. As a therapist, she believes that these types of support are an essential part of recovery for any family member affected by an addiction. Through therapy and Al-Anon, Carol began to understand how to create healthy boundaries, how to detach emotionally from Gregg's addiction, and how to take control of her own behavior and responses that were counterproductive to Gregg's recovery.

A YEAR LATER . . .

It takes an average of one year, after the onset of sufficiently motivating consequences, for most addicts to seek help. This was true for Gregg. Carol continued to treat Gregg with respect throughout the year, living apart (yet in the same home), retraining herself with healthy communication, and setting constructive boundaries.

After almost a year, Gregg was suffering consequences for his drinking in his business and health. Carol sought the counsel of pastors and godly friends for the next step. She came to the decision to separate, hoping Gregg would understand the depth of his illness. This was done while earnestly loving him and having his best at heart. Carol had assertively explained to Gregg how much it hurt her to watch him descend into the pit of addiction, and Gregg was aware of how much she truly loved him. Carol went to him with her decision and Gregg chose to cease drinking, and remains sober to this day.

Not all stories will end as successfully as Gregg and Carol's. Without a doubt, Carol attributes her ability to love Gregg unconditionally and choose a path that would lead to his recovery to the grace and power of God. Carol admits that she prayed fervently for selfless love for Gregg, knowing that this was God's will.

NOTE
1 Setting appropriate boundaries is further discussed in Dr. James C. Dobson, *Love Must Be Tough* (Wheaton: Tyndale House, 2007).

Reentry

Submission and the Often-Absent Husband

The wise woman builds her house,
but the foolish tears it down with her own hands.
—*Proverbs 14:1 NASB*

ON SEPTEMBER 17, 2001, Laura returned home from running errands. As she set her packages on her kitchen island, she noticed the red light blinking on her answering machine. She hit the Playback button and began unloading her groceries.

"Laura, this is David. By the time you receive this, I will be gone. I can't tell you where I'm going, and I don't know when I'll be back. I'll contact you as soon as I am able. I love you."

Laura sank into a chair and put her head in her hands. Although this was not unexpected, it still took her breath away. Laura's husband was in the military, in a special forces division. What should have been an easy assignment at the Pentagon had just turned into something quite different. A few days earlier, terrorists had attacked the United States, and now David's unit was sent into action.

David had gone on missions many times before, so Laura knew the drill. Because he was in special operations, he could not tell her many details of his mission. She knew he would keep his word and contact her as soon as he could, but she also knew that might be days, even weeks. In the meantime Laura lived by the axiom, "No news is good news."

Noticing the time of day, Laura returned to her groceries, realizing her children would soon walk into the house after school. She had things to do—homework, soccer practice, make dinner. . . .

WOMEN WITH A MISSION

Not all military wives are as adept at handling this kind of situation as Laura; however, I have observed that *successful* military wives have three traits in common. They are flexible, independent, and have a strong sense of mission. I have seen wives pack a home and move across country within two weeks. I have witnessed wives who deftly stepped into the life of a single parent as a spouse was stationed in a country deemed too dangerous for families. They have learned to take charge of their homes and their children when separated from their husband for as much as a year at a time.

Not to say that this is easy. However, their sense of mission gives them the strong will necessary to live under these uncertain and demanding conditions. One military wife told me, "Part of loving my country is letting my husband do his job."

I wondered how these women, with their characteristic independence, viewed their roles in marriage. What could they teach us about submission when their lives were often in flux as their husbands came in and out of the home? How did they support husbands whose careers took such a strong toll on the family?

I must admit that I also needed answers to this on a personal level. My husband's career causes him to travel a good deal of the time. It is not unusual for Michael to take six business trips in six weeks. Often these trips are for only two or three days; however, I am astounded by how many unexpected things can happen in that short span of time.

The most critical issue is always a decision concerning one of our kids. I am used to being part of a team where my husband is available to discuss discipline, boundaries, or even privileges for our children. I wondered what my military friends did to establish their husband's leadership in their home when he was often away on temporary duty.

IT'S ALL IN THE ATTITUDE

Tom was a naval aviator. He would be out at sea for six months at a time, flying missions from a floating landing strip aboard an aircraft carrier. This was before e-mail and cell phones, when communication was severely limited between the men serving on board these ships and their loved ones at home.

Fortunately for Tom, he married a wonderful woman who backed his choice of careers. Although I doubt Deshua understood what that would mean for their future, she wholeheartedly stepped into military life when she agreed to marry Tom.

Deshua will candidly admit that being separated from her husband for a long period of time was hard. Tom missed the births of two of their four children. He would be gone for three weeks, home for four days, gone for four weeks, home for three days. One year he was gone for a total of 270 days. Deshua realized that her attitude toward the navy would either hinder or help Tom in doing what he was called to do. She learned that, as his wife, she needed to give Tom permission to do his job. She related one circumstance that drove this point home to her.

"Tom called one evening right about dinnertime to let me know he would be late again. With a newborn and a toddler underfoot, I was looking forward to having my husband at home to help with the children and enjoy an evening together. As I walked toward the ringing phone, I instinctively knew who it would be and what he would say. I was tired, disappointed, and angry that Tom would need to stay at work when I needed to spend time with him.

"My first thought was to answer the phone and let him know how I felt, that being late wasn't acceptable, but before my hand reached the receiver, I felt God speaking to me. He reminded me that Tom wanted to be home just as much as I wanted him to be here, and Tom knew his call would disappoint me. I could either give Tom permission to do his job, and return home expectantly, or I could make it harder for him to enter the door, knowing he would face my anger.

"I realized my attitude would determine how Tom felt about coming home later. I wanted to create an atmosphere that Tom could not wait to return home to. Making him feel guilty about the demands of his job would not benefit either of us. So I made the decision to joyfully answer the phone."

BUILD A SIMILAR VISION

When Dad is frequently absent from their daily lives, it's easy for kids to forget that he is their authority. When her children were young, Deshua often included their father in daily activities even if he wasn't there. She would have the kids write Dad a letter, or draw a picture, or make a video—anything that would remind the kids that their father was part of the family.

Deshua wanted to help them understand that having a dad like Tom, who was willing to sacrifice for his country, was an honor and a privilege. She helped them focus on those things rather than feeling sorry that their dad missed their school play.

As their children grew older, Deshua and Tom realized their parenting strategies had to be defined and refined before Tom was sent on another assignment. When they worked together to hammer out boundaries or goals for each child, Deshua had a framework for making decisions that she knew Tom would agree with.

This also reminded the kids that their parents were a team. Deshua could say with full confidence, "Your father and I think . . ." and know Tom would support her decisions when he returned home. But to do this effectively, the children had to witness that teamwork while Tom was present. As in all families, there were times when Tom and Deshua did not agree on the right parenting style. However, they kept these differences to themselves and worked them out privately rather than in their kids' presence.

During these discussions Deshua said she made a point of trying to see the situation through Tom's perspective. She realized it was easy to focus on what Tom could do better, and avoid addressing her own weaknesses. They would talk with each other and ask, "What could I do differently? Was I too harsh or too permissive? How could we handle that next time?"

In taking this time to communicate, they achieved a unified front and the advantage of two parents working toward the same goal of raising godly children. It also reminded their kids that Tom was the biblical leader in the home, even when he was in the middle of an ocean.

A LESSON FROM SPACE

On the morning of February 1, 2003, the space shuttle Columbia broke up during reentry, more than 200,000 feet above Texas. The subsequent investigation revealed the cause of the accident. During liftoff, pieces of foam insulation fell off the external fuel tank and struck the left wing.

The insulation damaged the heat protection tiles on the wing. When Columbia reentered the atmosphere, hot gases entered the wing through the damaged area and melted the airframe. The shuttle lost control and broke up.

Reentry is also a critical time for military families. Even stable marriages experience stress after a spouse has had frequent or long periods of deployment. Communication and understanding these potential problems appear to be the best remedy against a meltdown.

Karen is married to a military officer who frequently travels throughout the world. I spoke with her about reentry and how she navigated her husband's return to family life.

Karen has observed two things that happen after her husband's initially happy reunion. First, her children continue to come to her for anything and everything, leaving her husband

Can You Be Too Independent?

Several years ago I learned an interesting lesson. My husband needed to be out of town to visit a friend with a serious illness. I was left at home with the kids, doing what I always do.

Usually this isn't a problem for me. However, this time I was struggling with eye problems that complicated my life. I could not see well enough to carry on my normal "mom" duties, and as the days passed I became increasingly frustrated. Nevertheless, knowing that my husband was needed at our friend's deathbed, I tried to hide my discomfort and refused to play the helpless woman stereotype.

After a week I was at the end of my rope. When Michael called one evening just before bedtime, I burst into tears.

"If Floyd isn't going to die, can you come home right away?" The words tumbled from my mouth before I could consider how harsh they sounded. Michael chuckled and promised to return on the next flight out.

I expected Michael to return home disappointed for

having to leave so suddenly. I apologized profusely, but he was adamant.

"Cindy, I will always be here if you need me. You are my first priority." To my surprise, he was happy to come home.

My lesson? Our husbands want to be needed. They <u>need</u> to be needed. For years I thought the best way to help my husband was to be a tower of strength and self-reliance. I was amazed to realize that my drive for independence kept my husband from filling his important, God-given role to care for me.

When I try to handle everything on my own, I send Michael the wrong message. As resourceful women, we need to guard against appearing so capable that we communicate self-sufficiency. After all, no man is an island. And a woman isn't either.

the odd man out. Second, she finds that her kids tend to play one parent off another, especially when they aren't getting what they want.

Karen found that reentry happens when Dad tries to regain his position as leader and the kids don't like what they hear. His control is challenged, and conflict results. For Karen, the helpmate of her husband, this moment is critical. She can either build her husband up, giving him back his position as head of the home, or she can undercut his authority.

Karen said she has to choose wisely by supporting him in front of the kids, encouraging him, and making him look good as the leader of the family. She found that sometimes her husband had incomplete information at the time of reentry. She would need to speak with her husband, out of the children's hearing, to fill him in on details that happened during his absence. Karen found she needed to consciously elevate her husband and his opinion. She realized that she held the power to restore order to the home upon her husband's return. With her words and actions, she could either celebrate his return to his rightful place or insert herself and upset the balance.

TAKING TIME TO RECONNECT

As I was ending my interview with one of my military friends, I asked her for any final words of advice. Her thoughts surprised me because they concerned an area of "willing cooperation" that I had not considered. She said that before a naval ship returns to port, the wives are given a briefing by the base staff. During this meeting they hear from commanders and staff counselors who explain common problems of reentry and how to make a smooth transition back into family life.

One of the issues they always raise is that of reestablishing a sexual relationship. Of course, most men returning from deployment are more than ready to be intimate with their wives. And legend has it that some wives will meet their husbands at the dock with a negligee under their coat and a Winnebago in the parking lot. But for others the lack of emotional connection can cause them to resist the immediate overtures of their husbands.

The simple advice of this military wife was to take time to reconnect. This may mean you need to spend your first night together away from the kids. Perhaps you can get a babysitter the first night your husband returns home, or send the kids to spend the night with friends. Set a romantic atmosphere. Go to a favorite restaurant or have a picnic in front of the fireplace. Express your expectations and your concerns, and let him discuss his.

In the final analysis, remember that physical intimacy is a primary love language of most men. As one wife said, "I love this man and this is what he needs."

Sex and Submission

One area of potential conflict in any marriage is in the sphere of the sexual relationship. Husbands and wives often have differing views toward sex, including the frequency and form of their love life.

Women need to understand how important sexual fulfillment is to their husband, and how much a physical relationship communicates respect to him.

On the other hand, a husband must never demand sex from his wife or require her to engage in acts that make her uncomfortable. It is important to note that God created our husbands with the desire for sex, and wives are the only legitimate outlet to have those needs met. In God's eyes, the sexual relationship in marriage is sacred.

Consider that The Song of Solomon, the twenty-second book in the Old Testament, is a picture of a loving relationship between a husband and wife. One of my favorite portions of this love story is in chapter 7:10–12 (NASB): "I am my beloved's, and his desire is for me. Come, my beloved, let us go out into the country, let us spend the night in the villages. Let us rise early and go to the vineyards. . . . There I will give you my love."

Three things pop out at me as I read this passage. First, the writer realizes her husband has a need and that she is the one who can meet it. ("I am my beloved's, and his desire is for me.")

Second, she makes a plan by inviting her husband to go away with her. ("Come, my beloved, let us go out into the country, let us spend the night in the villages.")

Finally, she initiates sex with him. ("Let us rise early and go to the vineyards. . . . There I will give you my love.") At the risk of being too shocking, I might also point out that Solomon's bride was willing to be somewhat adventurous in her choice of locations.

In the same way, our husbands would be very encouraged if we would enthusiastically meet their sexual needs. Plan a weekend away without the children. Take the initiative in making love. Show your husband you respect his longings and want to meet them. Realize that in responding to your husband's physical needs, you are building him up by letting him know you value him as a man.

7

The Power Broker

Submission in the Home of a Powerful Woman

For we are God's workmanship, created in Christ Jesus to do good works, which God prepared in advance for us to do.
—*Ephesians 2:10*

MONEY IS POWER. At least that's the theory in most of the world. Not so in Washington D.C. Inside the Beltway it's not what you know but who you know. It's not how much money you have but how much power you yield.

Janet Parshall knows everyone. In talk radio, she is a power broker. More than likely, you've heard Janet's voice over the airwaves as she hosts her nationally syndicated radio program *Janet Parshall's America.* Or you may have seen her face on Fox News, CNN, *Hardball, Larry King Live* or even in *People* magazine. Janet is an articulate spokesperson and an advocate for principles and policies that strengthen the family, and she's the smartest woman I know.

Raised in Wisconsin, Janet is the oldest of three siblings.

Her dad was a football coach and, in her eyes, the embodiment of strength and courage. His influence over his athletes reached much further than the limits of the field, and Janet watched her father turn teenage boys into men.

Janet's mom was a compassionate nurse, working first in the field of psychiatry and later as a hospice nurse, counseling families as they dealt with the death of a loved one. Both her mother and father were avid followers of Jesus Christ, and had their family involved in church several times each week.

As the oldest child, Janet exhibits many of the typical characteristics of a firstborn. She is conscientious, reliable, ambitious, and a natural leader. Her quest for knowledge was apparent even at a young age as she regularly attended activities at the nearby New Tribes Bible Institute. She spent hours sitting cross-legged on the concrete floor, listening to missionaries tell the stories of their lives in foreign lands. Having two younger brothers, and being confident in her faith, Janet was not easily intimidated by boys her age or afraid to stand for her beliefs. These traits were obvious the first time she set her eyes on Craig.

CONFRONTATION AT FIRST SIGHT . . .

"My senior year in high school, I was sitting in drama class at the front of the auditorium. In the back of the auditorium was this boy, surrounded by all the drama class beauties and giving a tutorial on relationships. He was explaining, as they sat wide-eyed in rapt attention, that in order to have a successful relationship you needed to know someone completely before you're married, including sexually."

This was the 1960s and the sexual revolution was in full swing. But Janet knew differently. Her parents had taught her the difference between good and evil, and she knew what this young man was espousing did not fit in the "good" category. Still, with heart pounding, she kept her head buried in her book, hoping someone would confront this fellow.

"But he kept going and going and I'm thinking, 'Hey, he's not only giving out his blather on what he believes, but he's influencing lives. Somebody better confront him,'" Janet explains. "So I'm waiting and waiting, and no one does it. So I turned around and said, 'Hey, that was sin when we walked out of the garden, it's a sin now, and it will always be a sin.' He straightened up in his chair and said, 'Can I walk you to your next class?'"

Janet's antennas went up immediately, knowing this was a guy she could not, and would not, be able to date. He was clearly not a follower of Christ, and she knew he might be trouble. When Craig asked to continue their conversation, Janet invited him over to sit on the front step of her house to talk. "In my mind this was not dating. We're talking and we're out there on the front step. The whole neighborhood can see me, nothing is going to happen, I'm not going to make any wrong choices. Well, I got in over my head because I didn't realize that this young man was brilliant."

Craig had been reading the philosophers, and was completely absorbed in their ideas. Janet would sit on the steps with him and listen to his worldview, thinking, *How do I respond to this?*

So she gave him the Campus Crusade brochure explaining the Four Spiritual Laws.[1] The next "step night," Craig was ready for more. Janet started feeding him the works of C. S. Lewis, beginning with *Mere Christianity*, followed by *The Screwtape Letters*, and *The Abolition of Man*, until she eventually exhausted the resources of her home library.

Finally, Craig reached the tipping point in his spiritual search. One evening he said, "OK, I'll believe this Jesus of yours if I can talk to someone who's communicated with the dead."

Janet had heard missionaries talk about encountering the occult and spiritualism in the darker regions of the world, so she knew that if anyone could help Craig with this last request, they would be at the New Tribes Bible Institute. She encouraged Craig to go to the institute to see if someone there could answer his question.

Craig did that the following Saturday. He met with the director of the institute, who listened until Craig emptied himself of every question. Then the director turned to the young man and said, "Now I have one for you. Where are you going when you die?"

Craig was stunned by this profound question. The existentialist philosophers he had read offered no hope of life after death but thought that death lead to nothingness. The prospect of eternal life with God was antithetical to this way of thinking. That day Craig decided to trust Christ with both his immediate and eternal future.

BABIES AND LEGAL BRIEFS

Janet and Craig married at the end of their junior year in college. As they approached graduation, Craig considered attending seminary. Both had a passion to serve Christ but were unsure of where that would lead them. However, several people counseled Craig to consider law school, because at the time there were no Christian civil rights groups fighting for religious rights.

The next few years Craig attended law school while Janet stayed at home raising their four children. This was not what Janet had expected. "I had been working on my master's degree in music for vocal performance. I was an opera singer, and thought I'd have this big career singing as a mezzo soprano in the opera while Craig was at law school."

By this time the feminist movement dominated women's thoughts. Almost nightly Janet turned on the news to see feminist leaders like Betty Friedan and Gloria Steinem espousing ridiculous phrases like, "Women need a man like a fish needs a bicycle," or "Your true worth and value can only be found in the workplace, not in the home."

As Janet looked around her neighborhood, she realized that many women were buying into this belief system. But Janet was not biting. She remembered the importance of investing in the future by raising her children well. Additionally, Craig continued to be very affirming of Janet's role as his wife and the mother of their kids.

Years later, Janet would reflect on this significant time in her life. "Women do lead lives different than men. We lead lives in seasons, and something is rich and precious and enduring in each one. In each season, God would inevitably teach me something that would be used in the following season. I don't think God would have called me to a pro-family organization if I hadn't had those years at home raising four kids. It would have been a hollow apologetic. I had to know the nitty-gritty of raising kids before I'd be allowed to work in public policy that would facilitate our raising kids."

During these years at home, Janet was also being groomed for her future role from an unexpected source. Craig would come home and hand her a legal brief. He'd say, "Honey, when the kids go down for a nap, I want you to read this brief, and then tonight after the kids are in bed, you tell me, as an attorney, whom you would pick for the jury and whom you would rule for in this case."

This process did two things for Janet. She was learning

to think critically in a season when she could have let her mind atrophy, and as she discussed the law with Craig, she was being wooed into his life.

STEPPING INTO THE CULTURE WARS

"As the kids grew up, we sent them to the local school a block away, the same school I had attended and taught in. The oldest came home one day and said, 'Mom we had an interesting day at school. They made us sit in a magic circle and they passed around a red scarf. When the scarf got to us, we had to answer three questions: Do you bite your nails, do you wet the bed, and if your parents divorced, who would you want to live with?'

"I honestly thought that the floor was going to open up and swallow me because every bit of training, teaching, praying, and nurturing that Craig and I have done for our children was now in the crosshairs of a cultural war that I didn't even know existed," Janet said. She was the PTA president. She thought that surely this was a misunderstanding and asked to check the curriculum. "What Craig and I discovered was that our elementary school had been chosen as an experimental site by the Department of Education for 'in class guidance counseling.' They wanted to use those invasive procedures to identify at-risk kids. In the process, of course, they trampled on the rights and privacy of families that were healthy and didn't need intervention."

This was Janet's introduction into the world of family advocacy as she and Craig began talking about their concerns with other parents. They were invited to speak at home church gatherings, at the local library, and all over the community.

The local Christian radio station invited Janet to speak on air about these issues. At the end of that interview, the station manager offered to let her host her own radio talk show. After determining that the show would not interfere with her family schedule, and with Craig's encouragement, Janet began her career in radio broadcasting.

Two years later, Janet moved her program to a larger radio station in Milwaukee. God used these opportunities to teach her to listen and to drive her to His Word as she searched Scriptures for the answers to her callers' questions.

Another consequence of Janet's experience with local school issues was her involvement with Concerned Women of America. Aware of the cultural battles around her, she volunteered at both the local and state levels before being asked to join the national board of CWA by Beverly LaHaye, the president of the organization. Janet helped represent Mrs. LaHaye and CWA to the major media, gaining national exposure in the process. Out of this, Janet received a phone call she never expected. She was invited to move to Washington

D.C., with the prospect of becoming the future president of Concerned Women of America.

"If I had been a raging feminist, I would have goose-stepped into the kitchen and said to my husband, 'God has called us to Washington, pack your bags.' But I knew that wasn't my role and I knew that wasn't right. I asked Craig, 'What do we do?' And he said, 'Janet, when God calls a couple, He calls them together. Let's wait and see what God does.'"

Exactly one week later, Craig received a call from John Whitehead of the Rutherford Institute, asking him to manage the East Coast office. Craig looked at Janet and said, "God doesn't have to shout; we heard Him loud and clear."

NATIONAL PROMINENCE

All of these experiences worked together to bring Janet to the place she is today: host of her own nationally syndicated daily talk show. Her intellect and verbal acumen have made her a popular commentator in the national media on issues concerning public policy. She has written several books, both fiction (with Craig as coauthor) and nonfiction.[2]

Janet's prominence has brought her celebrity status. It is not uncommon for people to stare when she walks into a crowded room, and many jockey for the chance to speak with her.

I asked how she dealt with that huge public persona. I wondered how she managed that in relation to her husband

and the head/helper roles in marriage. Janet laughed, saying, "Craig and I have discussed this again and again. He understands that this is part of the work I was called to do. What Craig sees that others don't is my sweaty palms and knocking knees before I walk in the room. He knows that before we left home I had to throw the sheets in the dryer and write a check for the dry cleaners. Craig understands that part of my ministry is to be a role model. The 'people want to talk to you thing' is part of that, it's the Titus 2 thing."

Janet also pointed out that, by God's providence, her work has always connected with Craig's. He is a well-known Christian civil liberties attorney and the senior vice president and general counsel of the National Religious Broadcasters Association. Craig has authored numerous legal-suspense novels, is a magazine columnist, and speaks nationally on legal and worldview issues. Because of Craig's expertise, she often has him share her microphone. "I've told Craig that beyond the content of religious legislation and how that impacts the family, the audience is listening to how we interact, how we laugh, how we speak to each other, and I think there is a witnessing tool in all of this. I think this is about showing a healthy marriage to a country that is divorce minded."

Being Boss in the Marketplace

In the process of interviewing for this project, I spoke with several women who were supervisors in their workplace. Many of them offered their insights into being a female boss. The consensus was that the "I am woman, hear me roar" mentality was not helpful as either an employer or employee. These women saw their roles as developing their staffs, leading by example, rather than being domineering or punitive.

They carefully made sure that their leadership style was never demeaning. A female boss should be confident in her abilities, but gracious in the way she communicates her directives. She should never confuse aggressiveness with strength. Women who feel they have something to prove to their male counterparts will quickly lose the respect they need to lead a team.

Regardless of your position in the marketplace, you are an ambassador for Christ. Your first priority should be to represent Christ well, and to lead in a way that will honor Him.

THE PARABLE OF THE TREES AND PETER PAN

Janet likens her relationship with Craig to two trees growing in their yard. "We have a tree with a sapling that is completely wrapped around the tree. It's like someone artistically designed it. That is my picture of my relationship with Craig. I really can't tell you where one tree stops and the other tree begins."

It's the same in their marriage. "Every time the path has made another turn, it has absolutely been in harmony and parallel to what God is calling Craig to do. It's been an easy progress for me because my little branch is wrapping around the base of his life, and whichever way his tree is swaying, I just naturally sway in the wind at the same time so it's not an overarching, constant struggle."

Janet gives Craig much of the credit for her personal accomplishments. "I often refer to Craig as my Peter Pan. He would sprinkle fairy dust and say 'fly.' When I was afraid to even step on the window ledge like Wendy, Craig would say, 'You can do this.' At times I'd be called to debate feminists on the stage in New York and I'd tell Craig, 'I'd rather have a root canal,' and he would say, 'You can do this. In your weakness God is made strong.' Craig would embolden me. He would say, 'Fly, Wendy, you can fly.'"

BEING JANET PARSHALL

I asked Janet how she balanced being the boss of the workplace with being in the role of helper at home. "It's an interesting dualism in my life. I am the one calling the shots because that's the definer of what I do in the workplace, but it's definitely not the definer of what I do when I come home. I'm in a supervisory position at work, but that is something I have to shed on the commute home. I can't think of a faster prescription for chaos in our marriage."

Janet believes God prepared her slowly, incrementally for this dual role. Her broadcasting career has never been her first priority. "My primary identity is not as a broadcaster but as the wife of Craig and the mother to our children. Feminists say, 'You can have it all.' But they practice the sin of omission. You should say, 'You can have it all—but you can't have it all at the same time.' We women have to make choices, but we don't get a second chance. If you miss the first step or that first word or that birthday party, you don't get a redo."

Clearly, Janet admires and respects her husband, but she was concerned that readers weren't left thinking she had a perfect marriage. "I like to say that marriage, on its face, is an absolutely ludicrous idea. To put two sinners together under one roof and say, 'Now live happily ever after' . . . it shouldn't work. If you take our rebellious nature, if you take our sinful nature, we should be clawing at each other constantly. The fact that marriage works at all is because we have to be in relationship with one another as God defined."

It starts with loving the Lord. "If you don't honor and love Him, then you won't be able, in your own flesh, to love and submit to your husband in the way God calls us to. First start by loving God so completely, so utterly, that you want to step into His good and perfect will . . . and His good and perfect will is that you love your husband with an unconditional and submissive posture."

Many problems in marriage can be whittled down to a single factor: pride. There have been times when Craig and Janet did not agree, and Craig would let Janet do it her way. "There would be utter dissatisfaction in my mouth. I got my way, but I didn't have my husband's support, and it probably wasn't the right choice in those set of circumstances. In the end all I had was my pride, and pride is very unsatisfying because it is like an addiction. All pride wants is to be fed and it is never satisfied." Janet continued, "After thirty-seven years of marriage, it still has to be moment by moment, because flesh rears its ugly head. Because self says, 'I'm gonna push God off the throne.' Because 'me' says, 'I still should be first.'

"You have to learn that even if you fall down, even if you have a day where your marriage just stunk, it is wonderful to know we serve a God of second chances and fresh starts. We wake up with a clean slate no matter how much we've blown it the day before. I don't know a husband out there who doesn't want his wife to love him unconditionally, and I don't know a wife out there who doesn't want her husband to love her like Christ loved the church. It just doesn't get any better than that."

NOTES
1. See appendix 2 for an explanation of the Four Spiritual Laws.

2. For more information check out jpamerica.com.

The Wage Earner

Submission and Economic Role Reversal

She considers a field and buys it; from her earnings she plants a vineyard. . . . She senses that her gain is good; her lamp does not go out at night.

— *Proverbs 31:16, 18 NASB*

VICKI'S MOTHER'S best friend approached her and stated, "If you let him have his way, you'll never get your way again."

Vicki thought that was an odd thing to say to a bride on her wedding day. Stranger still, the woman attended a church where the list of dos and don'ts was set in stone, and one thing high on the list was that women were to obey their husbands. Thirty-nine years later Vicki still remembers the words and the effect they had on her heart.

She also remembers the consequences that attending that particular legalistic church had on her early years of marriage. When Jim and Vicki married, they didn't realize there was a biblical model for marriage. In their church, spirituality was defined by a set of rules. They learned that Jim was the master of the house, and Vicki was to unquestioningly comply with his desires. Both Jim and Vicki were strong willed, and both desired a sense of control. Obviously the whole idea of submission was difficult to work out in their home.

Because of what they were taught in the church, Jim led by telling Vicki what to do. She submitted in a way that would still achieve her desired results. This pattern of demand and manipulation was not broken until after Jim and Vicki reached an impasse in their thirteen-year marriage that brought them into counseling. Vicki returned home after one counseling session and told Jim, "I'm done. If I don't feel like doing something, I'm not doing it. I'm not playing games anymore, I'm not manipulating."

Jim loved Vicki enough to admit, "Maybe I blew it . . . let's work on this."

Today, Vicki and Jim's marriage is on solid footing. "We are still both strong willed, and we still have control issues," Vicki says. But they have gained the wisdom of knowing each other's strengths. "Jim is better in some areas. He also knows there are things I'm better at than he is. We didn't start this way . . . we are still a work in progress." Their mutual respect has given Vicki permission to succeed in business without making Jim feeling threatened.

Legalistic Submission

Years ago my husband and I entertained guests in our home. Our plan was to take them out to dinner, but at the last minute my husband was needed at work. Not wanting to waste our reservations, I took the couple out on my own. Later in the evening, the male guest pulled my husband aside, very concerned that I was not a "submissive, feminine woman." Apparently, he decided that because I chose where we would sit in the restaurant.

I was stunned by this view of submission. My motives for selecting our seats were based on the fact that I knew the layout of the establishment and the quietest table for conversation. Regardless, this man was not my husband, and I was not obligated to submit to his need for control.

Biblical submission is from the heart, rather than an outward conformity to a set of rules. When we begin defining submission by what we should or should not do, we are falling into the trap of legalism. Legalism may lead to the abuse of power by the one in authority, because the rule becomes more important than the sincerity of the follower. Outward compliance to a set of rules will eventually breed anger and bitterness.

God's divine plan for our roles in marriage was given to benefit the relationship, not the individual. When either spouse sees his or her position as personally advantageous, he or she is not living out the relationship as God intended. The focus of the husband should be to love his wife like Christ loved the church, which requires sacrifice. The motivation behind biblical submission is for us wives to follow our husbands in a way that will honor Christ.

HER MIDLIFE CRISIS

Their youngest child was in kindergarten. Vicki was thirty-eight years old, and feeling restless. She was doing an increasing amount of volunteer work for the navy, and decided if she was going to stay that busy, she might as well get paid for it.

However, Vicki wanted flexibility. Her family was still her first priority, so she began to consider careers that would be profitable, while accommodating her children's needs.

Jim was a military officer with good pay and benefits, which meant Vicki didn't have to worry about a fixed income or health care. In the end, she chose the field of real estate. I remember telling Jim, "My goal is to make more money than you make."

He was a wise man and said, "I'll back you in that."

Jim never felt threatened and wanted Vicki to succeed.

Twenty years later Jim retired from the military. Vicki was concerned because this meant a large reduction in the monthly income. Although Vicki was doing well in a strong housing market, her salary was commission only. Subsequently, she felt the added pressure of needing to provide a consistent income at the preretirement level.

Before retiring, Jim got his real estate license, was managing several rental properties for out-of-state clients, and finished training in real estate appraisal. But Vicki desperately wanted Jim to have a corporate job with the salary and benefits he had enjoyed in the military. They agreed that it would take Jim three years to establish his business.

Vicki never wanted to be the primary wage earner. "I cried on every anniversary of his retirement from the military," she says. "But every year the Lord would say to me, 'Haven't I taken care of you?' Jim offered to get a corporate job if I wanted him to, but God had already reminded me that He would provide our needs."

Vicki knew she could trust Jim's leadership and chose to

defer to his aspirations, realizing that by yielding to Jim, she was placing herself under God's protection. "By the third year I loved it. It was a perfect fit."

Jim was a successful appraiser, property manager, and also provided the support work in real estate while Vicki remained the "face" of the team.

To Work or Not to Work

Ever since women joined the workforce, we have faced the question of whether to work outside the home or not. For some families this is an easy issue. Many mothers choose to stay home with their young children, some even giving up lucrative careers to do so.

However, for some women it is not a choice. Economic circumstances may force a mother into the employment lines when she would prefer to remain at home. Still others cannot imagine life without a career. When facing the question of whether to work outside the home or not, it's helpful to keep a few things in mind:

- Before having children, don't become dependent on your income. As much as you love your career, your feelings may change when you hold your baby in your arms. Give yourself the freedom to still have a choice when you have a family.

- If you do have children, keep them as your first priority. It takes a great deal of time and energy to raise a child. Don't try to be all things to all people. You really can't have it all at the same time. Look at your life as chapters of a long book, rather than a short story.

- Don't let our culture lie to you. You really can live off of one income if you make sound financial decisions. This means spending less than you earn. You may be much happier in a smaller home with an older car than trying to juggle it all and becoming physically and emotionally exhausted.

- If you choose to work, remember your job is not your legacy. Future generations may not remember what you did, or how much you earned, but they will know the impact you had on your husband and children.

BEEN THERE, DONE THAT

I know from my own experience that a reversal in economic earning power can cause a subtle shift in marital roles. When my husband and I were in our early years of marriage, Michael was in a four-year graduate program. We considered this his full-time work. He took on part-time jobs, mainly manual labor, to pay his tuition and help ends meet in lean months. I was employed in the banking industry during those years and was the primary wage earner, working full-time until the day I gave birth to our first child.

After I left my salaried career, I realized that we had experienced a slight reversal in our roles. I had become very concerned over how "the money I had earned" was being spent. I felt a sense of power that did not reflect respect for my husband and the effort he was putting into his education. I've learned that other women in similar circumstances encounter the same feelings I had.

At marriage conferences, women who earn higher salaries than their husbands often approach me. They are concerned that the income disparity does not become an issue in their marriage. Unfortunately, our society equates earning power with success. Try as we might, our culture does affect the way we view ourselves and our home lives. It also influences our neighbors' opinions of us.

With this in mind, I asked Vicki for advice. I wondered

what she would say to a young woman who believed in the biblical model of submission and was uneasy about the effects of this role reversal on her marriage.

1. *Don't make it about you.* Vicki told me that she had been counseled to take her name off of her business. It wasn't "Vicki and . . ." Although she is the face of the real estate team, she isn't the head of the team. Vicki told me "it is the best single piece of advice I've ever received." Doing this kept Jim from being put in the background in other people's minds.

2. *Have honest conversation with your husband.* Discuss how he will feel if you make more money than he does. Thoroughly examine your own feelings. How will you feel making more money than your husband? Will you lord it over him? "You may have more earning potential, but he may be affecting people in more important ways. Both of you matter. Your marriage has to be so open because anything can get in there and dig away at your relationship," Vicki says.

3. *Always refer to* our *money, not* my *money.* He must have a part in it. You can't do whatever you do without his support. Jim gives Vicki invaluable assistance in marketing and technical support. If your husband cannot have a hands-on responsibility in your career, be humbly aware of every sacrifice he makes that allows you to succeed.

4. *Give your husband leadership in the financial arena.* This doesn't mean he writes each check or pays each bill. It does mean you follow his leadership in allocating your resources. "We decide how to divide every one of my checks together," Vicki says. Discuss how much you will budget for savings, spending, and tithing. Always maintain joint accounts. One way Vicki acknowledges Jim's leadership is by always seeking his consent before big spending decisions. "Jim has always given me permission to spend, but often I don't, because money isn't important . . . we have enough, so spending isn't an issue anymore."

5. *Always show your husband respect in public.* "Jim knows I respect him because I never criticize him in front of others. If I have an issue to discuss, I always do it in private," Vicki says. Your friends and colleagues will tune in to your attitude toward your husband, which will either build him up or tear him down as they view him through your eyes.

6. *Acknowledge his leadership in front of your children.* "I made the mistake of correcting Jim in front of my kids. It's not the way to do it. I regret that," Vicki admits. As women we sometimes have insights into our children that our husbands lack. But the same is true for our husbands. We need to discuss our parenting behind closed doors, so we walk out of those doors as a united front.

The Power of "10"

Sometimes in trying to communicate with our husbands, we send mixed signals about what we really want and feel. To help alleviate this, Jim and Vicki have instituted a scale system when faced with a decision. This works for small decisions (i.e., "Do you want to eat dinner out or at home?") and big decisions. Simply ask the question: "On a scale of 1–10, how much do you want to do this?"

Vicki realized "we often do things because we think the other person wants to do it, when they really don't. This system helps you identify what you really think and want."

Vicki acknowledged that if Jim had been threatened by her earning potential, she would not have gone into real estate. Her marriage was more important than her income. "I don't know why I said I wanted to make more money than Jim," she explains. "I didn't feel like I was going to be in competition with him. I just had a goal in mind. I don't think I needed to feel equal. I never felt like a doormat or like I wasn't worthwhile."

Taking the Focus off Money

Years ago my husband and I were asked to join some wealthier friends on a European vacation. After discussing the trip, including time away from our small children and the expense of travel, we decided to pass on the excursion. When our friend phoned to inquire about our decision, I innocently said, "Thanks, but we just don't have the money right now."

Later in the evening, I mentioned the call to Michael. As soon as the words were out of my mouth, Michael's countenance fell, and I knew I had said something wrong.

"OK, I'm confused," I said. "I thought we agreed not to go."

"We did, Cindy, but not because we don't have enough money. We have that amount in the bank, but we decided to use those funds in a different way."

Michael was right, of course. We did have what we needed for the vacation, but not enough for the trip and a down payment for a house we hoped to purchase.

For the first time I understood that how I talked

about money affected the way my husband viewed himself. If we "didn't have enough," then Michael felt inadequate as a provider.

Even when you are the primary wage earner in your home, your husband still has an innate need to provide. As a result, it's even more important that your salary is never compared to his, or discussed in a way that makes him feel inadequate.

Take the focus off money. Instead, keep it on the passion you each have for your careers, and how you are both making contributions in different ways. Encourage your husband in his roles outside of employment, like his involvement with your children or in your community. In the end, how much we make is of little importance. The influence we have, especially on those we love, will have lasting impact.

Culture Battles

Submission and Matriarchy

And do not be conformed to this world, but be transformed by the renewing of your mind, so that you may prove what the will of God is, that which is good, and acceptable and perfect.
— *Romans 12:2 NASB*

"BLACK WOMEN are raised from a young age to be very strong, with the notion that you might not have a man to take care of you. You might have to get out in the world and make it on your own. Part of it is protection, you don't want to be ill-prepared . . . needy . . . expecting some man to come along as your knight in shining armor, because that just doesn't happen for many of us. The goal that is held up for black women is to become self-sufficient, make tons of money, and provide for yourself."

I was sitting with Katherine in a local deli as she described the culture in which she was raised. Katherine's mother was a strong willed, smart, and accomplished woman. She raised her daughters to be the same: formidable and independent. The girls learned that to get ahead you couldn't just be good; you had to be better than everyone else. Her mother's ideals were for her daughters to be educated and intelligent.

In contrast, Katherine's stepfather was emotionally and sexually abusive to the girls. He would demean them by saying things like, "When you grow up you'll be eating the bark off trees."

He frequently had fits of rage, often cursing at the girls, but never in front of their mother. Ironically, Katherine's stepfather was a deacon in the local church and was considered to be a pillar of the community. Katherine noted the contradiction in his private and pubic persona. She learned to distrust men and their leadership. She internalized all of this by working harder than others, being driven toward perfection.

As a result, by the time she left for college, Katherine was an enthusiastic feminist. She intentionally chose to major in a male-dominated field, and she was well qualified, equipped to get along with men, to compete on their level. She would prove that she did not need a man. Katherine could certainly take care of herself.

Then she met Thomas.

HER PARADIGM SHIFT

Thomas approached Katherine at a campus bus stop. He was a graduate student; she, a freshman. He struck up a conversation that lasted for their short bus ride. A week later she ran into Thomas in the student union. Soon after, they went on their first date to a movie and ended their evening by talking for hours. "I shared things with Thomas that I'd never shared before. He was very attentive as I told him some very hard things," she recalls.

Katherine discovered they both loved God and wanted to be committed to Him. By the end of the evening, Thomas asked, "So when are we getting married?"

When Katherine left home, she had also left the church. It was impossible to reconcile her stepfather's abuse with his leadership in their local congregation. It gave her a bad taste for all things "religious." However, even her stepfather could not dampen her love for God. When she was young, Katherine often talked to God, calling Him "Daddy." Somewhere in her spirit she was able to separate the sinfulness of her stepfather from the truth of God's Word. Katherine knew God was someone to whom she could tell her secrets. Even in the atmosphere of abuse, Katherine was able to enjoy intimacy with her Lord.

But now Katherine felt she was being called back to the church. And that was OK. She and Thomas both wanted to center their relationship in Christ, and that would include going to church together.

Abuse and Authority . . . the Devastating Effect of Evil

Women who have been victimized as children often have trust issues with authority figures such as parents, husbands, pastors, bosses, and even God. They may also have problems developing and maintaining close personal relationships.

Often these women have distorted assumptions about true godly submission. They associate the word "submit" with being a doormat or a rag doll to be tossed around and thrown aside.

Victims of abuse may be angry or afraid of being put in a position of submission that may leave them feeling vulnerable. Experience has taught them not to trust; however, at some level, they desperately want to be able to trust and live out that trust in their adult relationships.

Concerning submission in marriage, it is important for women with this history to understand how past experiences affect their ability to connect with their husbands and trust in God's goodness and sovereignty. They must recognize their new identity in Christ, with all the privileges of being the daughter of a perfect and loving heavenly Father who will never leave or forsake them. Through this new identity they must overcome feelings of worthlessness and shame brought on by abuse. In addition, it is vital they comprehend that God's plan is for any authority figures in their lives to be loving and protective.

Those who have been wounded must differentiate between trust in man and trust in God. This often involves a process of examining old core beliefs and distorted thinking associated with those traumatic relationships, and then challenging them with the truth of God's Word. Trauma sufferers must begin to see the Lord as trustworthy in order to feel secure and submit "as unto the Lord."

God has the power to deliver us from these old identities. When we experience His love, we love others in deeper ways. When we experience the fullness of His grace, we can forgive others and offer them the grace we have received. This is an important place of godly empowerment for any victim. God's desire is for women to move beyond victimization and see themselves as His daughters: precious treasures, heirs of His promises, loved beyond measure, and righteous and clean in His sight through the blood of Jesus Christ.

—Cynthia Morris, MSW

The young couple wanted to do the right thing in their marriage, but because both came from dysfunctional families, they didn't have a clue how to do that. "Where do you go to find out how to be a good wife? A good parent? When you can't go to your family of origin, where do you go?" Katherine notes. They decided to go to God's Word and use it, literally, as a guide in marriage and parenting.

Katherine was a feminist until Thomas opened up the Bible. "When he read Ephesians 5:22–23 to me, I was angry. I didn't know enough about Scripture to know what it says about a husband's role in marriage or I would have argued the point with him.

"I was frustrated. I was angry at God because I didn't have a real high opinion of men, and the idea of a wife having to submit to a husband angered me. It was unfair. It didn't make sense."

Katherine decided she had to read the Scriptures for herself to find something that could contradict this. Perhaps Paul misspoke. So she began to dig.

THE CHALLENGE, THE CONCLUSION, THE CONFESSION

Katherine began to study the Word of God and pray. She challenged the Lord. She had gained intimacy with

God as a child, and now she went back to Him with that same determination.

"I don't believe You really mean this. It doesn't resonate with me," she told Him. "I don't like it. I don't feel good about it. It makes me feel less—not as intelligent, not as qualified, not as equipped, and I don't like that feeling."

After Katherine stopped ranting and raving before God, she felt His answer in her spirit. God said, "Katherine, it's not a question of whether you like it. It's not even a question of whether you like Thomas. It's a question of whether you love Me and will allow My Word to be preeminent in your life or not."

At that moment, Katherine knew what was expected of her. She didn't have to understand it. It didn't have to make rational sense. It didn't even have to feel fair. "I just needed to know that God said it, and if He said it, I just had to hang in there with submission long enough for the light to come on and for me to begin to feel it."

But what did submission look like? To Thomas, submission seemed to mean that Katherine should work all day, and then come home to make dinner and set it before him and clean up the dishes while he continued his full-time studies.

Katherine felt that Thomas didn't understand that he had a responsibility as head of the home to love her like Christ loved the church. It didn't look as if he even cared to know. But Katherine continued to grapple with the idea of submission, wondering how she could own it.

"I finally just settled it between me and the Lord," Katherine told me over lunch. "I didn't feel it, but I decided I would serve my husband and love him the way God wanted me to. I trusted that in His own time, God would turn the light on so Thomas would see that something was required of him."

Matriarchy in the African-American Culture

Dear Cindy,

I've thought much about our time last week and the issue of submission in the African-American culture. Thomas and I also talked about it, and I think it might be helpful to provide some historical background and foundation for the concept of matriarchy in the African-American culture.

The African-American culture hasn't arrived at a place where women are so strong or domineering because it was advantageous or seen as a positive. It has happened more as a default and a matter of survival.

I'm not sure how far it's helpful to go back, but

as recent as the Roosevelt years and the New Deal (1933–1939), black women were told that they could not receive government assistance if their husbands were in the home. This act destroyed families and forced women/mothers to choose between having their husbands in the home and being able to provide for their children.

Years later, with the advent of affirmative action, companies could hire an African-American woman and satisfy quotas for hiring a female and for hiring a minority at the same time. Each of these events served to minimize the importance of the African-American man in the home and to strip him of his key role of providing for his family. And they, in turn, positioned the African-American woman as the stronger party in leading and providing for her family.

Katherine

ME FIRST

"I really believe that for this thing to work the way the Lord wants it to, somebody has to do their part first. Wives are so reticent to submit because we are afraid of being taken advantage of. We say, 'What about him?' But there's a certain amount of freedom, because all of this is a faith issue."

Katherine makes a valid point. The question of submission is really one that asks, "Do I trust God enough to take Him at His word and to believe that His Word is not only the truth but *the truth of my life*?" If we do, then our responsibility as wives is to live it regardless of whether our husbands ever get it right or not.

Several years into the marriage, Katherine began to notice a change in Thomas. It first happened when she returned from a long day of church work. When she walked in the front door, Thomas had Katherine's robe waiting. He had run a hot bath, complete with bubbles. After soaking in a hot tub,

Submission and the African-American Church

Submission is almost a four-letter word in the black culture. The idea of submitting to a man is almost responded to violently by our women. I think because there are so many stories of abuse, absent fathers, and desertion. We don't have nearly enough stories of men who fulfill the biblical role of husband in our culture, so the idea of submitting is not talked about—hardly ever—even in the context of church."

Katherine has been given a national platform to speak on the role of women in the black church. She's discovered that often men need to be given permission to lead. "We need to allow men to lead, enabling and empowering their leadership."

This is even more critical in a church often overrun by women. "We need to facilitate male leadership by being still, giving them time to think, and affirming them as they lead our congregations."

But Katherine also points out that women, not men, must be the ones to spread this message in our churches. "A gentleman spoke on this at a conference and half the women walked out," she recalls.

However, when Katherine approaches the subject, she finds that women are surprisingly open to hearing what God's Word has to say. Most women long to understand what God has to say, even when it is difficult to hear. "There is a new awakening in our community to the topic of biblical manhood and biblical womanhood. As more of our men embrace their roles of godly, servant leadership, women are taking up the mantle of biblical womanhood."

Katherine entered the bedroom to find a table set with candles, and a wonderful meal of steak, baked potatoes, and salad, which Thomas had prepared. Suspicious of his attention, Katherine wondered if he was priming her for bad news. But his explanation was simple, "I just want you to know that I love you."

YEARS LATER . . .

"I still struggle with it all these years later," Katherine says, admitting that submission has never become part of her nature. But that makes sense to her in light of Scripture. "It's within us to want to lead and question our husbands on leadership. I wrestle with how to tame that part of myself that flares up again and again."

The area of finances has been one of Katherine's most difficult arenas for submission. "I am a saver, but Thomas is generous to a fault. He would give someone the shirt off his back. He feels personally responsible to meet another person's needs. I am the other extreme."

Katherine wanted to put money away for future expenses, like their children's college education. She would watch Thomas's generosity deplete their savings. Certainly his charity pleased God, but it often caused a marital rift. Katherine eventually learned that God would meet their needs if she would cooperate with her husband. Looking back, she has witnessed

God's faithfulness as every one of her children attended college without debt.

One of the strategies Katherine has learned is to communicate clearly with Thomas. At times she believes she is encouraging and affirming his leadership, yet he does not feel her support. Katherine has learned that attentive listening is not enough. She needs to hear what Thomas says, and then verbally encourage him. It sometimes helps for her to repeat Thomas's words back to him.

Like many husbands, Thomas often hears a few words of criticism much louder than many words of encouragement. "I'm learning that part of submission is to be a real affirmer, to be a cheerleader, learning to really speak in a way that is meaningful to my husband," Katherine says.

DON'T BE CONFORMED TO THIS WORLD. . . .

The journey to submission can be lonely, especially in a culture that offers no support. The modern woman would never embrace a choice to submit if left on her own. Wives who choose this role will never be understood by a culture that is absorbed with individual rights.

We may not even find support for submission in most churches, even those that profess to believe in the literal interpretation of the Scriptures. Regardless, this is what we are called to do.

A. W. Tozer addressed the loneliness of standing firm in this way. He said, "Most of the world's greatest souls have been lonely. Loneliness seems to be the price a saint must pay for his saintliness. The leader must be a man or a woman who, while welcoming the friendship and support of all who can offer it, has sufficient inner resources to stand alone, even in the face of fierce opposition, in the discharge of his responsibilities. They must be prepared to have no one but God."[1]

NOTE
1. A. W. Tozer, *The Pursuit of God* (Camp Hill, PA: Christian Publications, 1982), 145.

He Said . . .

What Our Husbands Think about Respect

However, each one of you also must love his wife as he loves himself, and the wife must respect her husband.
—*Ephesians 5:33*

ONE THING I'VE learned from having a son is that men and women really are different. Of course, I knew this from my own marriage, but comparing my son to my three daughters truly defines how our gender affects the way we perceive the world around us.

The girls in my home all think similarly. We have distinctive personalities, yet we tend to look at the world the same way. As I wrapped up this book, I wondered if I had missed anything. I learned something from every woman I interviewed. I gained new insights about what submission and respect looked like in a variety of marriages. Certainly, everything I heard had the ring of truth. But I was interested in knowing if our husbands would agree with our thinking, or shake their heads at how easily we could miss the mark. So I decided to ask them.

I sent a survey to three different groups of men from a variety of backgrounds, ages, and marriage lengths. The one thing they had in common was that they all professed to be followers of Jesus Christ and appeared to have fairly solid relationships with their wives. I wanted to see what men from good marriages would say about respect and leadership in their home. I asked them to complete these statements:

1. I wish my wife understood that ...
2. I know my wife respects me when ...
3. I don't feel respected when my wife ...

I asked the men to give me their immediate feedback to these statements. I expected a variety of answers. After all, these men represented different walks of life. Instead, the men shared many of the same concerns. A common thread consistently ran through their responses.

RESPECTFUL COMMUNICATION

If you ask a roomful of people the ingredients of a successful marriage, most of them will include good communication. Apparently, our husbands see the way we communicate with them as a primary source of respect. The following responses are a good representation of the men surveyed:

I wish that my wife understood that . . .

- I can't read her mind. I need her to tell me what she is thinking.
- When I ask her a question like, "What's for dinner?" I'm not saying, "What's wrong with you? Why isn't dinner ready?" I'm just asking if I should pick dinner up on the way home.
- When she says, "I just do" (when asked why she feels a certain way), it reminds me of my parents saying, "I just said so." It's a cop-out.
- When my wife is upset she seems to think she is not responsible for her words or actions. This temporarily erodes my trust in her.
- I have feelings too, even if I don't express them well.

I know my wife respects me when . . .

- I am wrong and she responds kindly.
- When she initiates a conversation with me about how I might have offended her or hurt her, and in doing so she does it in a way that is respectful instead of screaming at me or calling me names . . . etc.

• She is interested and engaged in what I have to say.

I don't feel respected when my wife . . .

• Walks out in the middle of a conflict rather than saying she needs time to think.
• Rolls her eyes at me when I'm speaking to her.
• Won't tell me what's bothering her, even when I ask.
• Does not listen well.
• Disregards my feelings.

Without a doubt, men and women communicate differently, which is one reason effective communication may be one of the biggest struggles in marriage. When Michael and I were newlyweds, I often reacted to him as if he were my father. Because my father had an erratic temper, I had avoided conflict with him at all costs. So in marriage, I would hide my feelings from Michael. Of course, he always knew when something was wrong, but I would deny it, and he would end up frustrated. I had to learn to express my feelings and trust that he would not be angry. Simply learning to tell Michael what bothered me was a huge step in our ability to resolve any problem.

Fortunately, we had received good premarital counseling that encouraged us to never use words that we would later regret. Michael and I agreed that we would never resort to name-calling or any other disparaging remark. Not that we don't make mistakes in our "discussions," but we work hard on focusing on the problem rather than the person. Attacking your spouse (verbally or otherwise) will always exacerbate the conflict. Using hurtful words is disrespectful in any relationship.

Another common theme in communication seems to be our unwillingness to take our husbands' words as they were meant. Sometimes we react to *what we think they said*, rather than what they did say. It's important to ask for clarification. Simple phrases like, "What I hear you saying is . . ." can easily diffuse a potential argument by giving husbands the chance to communicate clearly.

Look again at the previous responses to "I know my wife respects me when . . ." Our husbands appreciate when we express how we feel with kind words. They really do want to know when we are upset or hurt, but they also want the benefit of the doubt that they didn't intend to cause our distress. Speaking graciously communicates respect to our men.

Several husbands acknowledged that they didn't understand their wives' emotions. Even my junior high son complains about the emotional drama surrounding girls his age. Most boys simply don't live at an emotional level. Men tend to prefer facts over feelings in working through a problem. When we need to communicate a concern with our husbands, it is helpful to rehearse the facts so we don't let our emotions cloud the issue. I've learned to wait several days to speak with

Michael if I'm concerned about something in our relationship. That gives me time to be more objective and to think through my word choice to assure that I communicate clearly, honestly, and respectfully. Doing so gives me the best chance of being heard and understood.

But understanding goes both ways. Men in the survey indicated that they don't always sense that their wives understand or acknowledge their feelings. Our husbands' feelings are valid even if they don't agree with our own. The men in our lives may have been raised by the adage "Big boys don't cry." They may have a harder time accessing their emotions than we do. As a result, it is imperative that when your husband expresses his feelings, you never dismiss them. Instead, let him know that you hear his heart and empathize. Giving your husband the freedom to express himself emotionally, at his own comfort level, is a key to respectful communication.

RESPECT IN THE BEDROOM

Most men consider their sexual relationship with their wife to be a high priority. However, it might surprise you to learn that your husband's sexual fulfillment is fundamental to his need for respect. According to my survey, many men don't feel respect from their wives when the women withhold sex. Conversely, men know they're respected when their wives enjoy the sexual component of their relationship, especially when she initiates sexual intimacy.

As wives, we cannot underestimate the importance of the sexual relationship we have with our husband. A woman's need to connect with her husband emotionally is equivalent to his need to bond with her sexually. If our men constantly ignored us, our self-esteem would unravel. In the same way, a man's self-worth is in danger when we ignore his needs for intimacy.

One woman shared the following story with me. Her husband walked in the door after work. Toys were scattered all over the house, compliments of her three preschool children who'd played hard all day. Usually she tried to pick up before her husband arrived, but time had gotten away from her. Her husband was tired and frustrated as he gingerly stepped through the obstacle course. "It looks like a tornado went through this room. What have you done all day?"

Now, let me pause this scene for a moment. Most of us would have stopped our husbands cold, reminding them that being home all day with children was much harder than leaving each morning for a cushy job. We would have hubby in his place until he slunk back to the bedroom to change out of his work clothes.

Not my friend. She took an entirely different approach. She saw her husband was exhausted and needed revival. Setting her own needs aside, she chose to care for him rather than react. Making sure her children were occupied, she pulled her husband into the powder room and made love to him. Happy man. Smart woman. He never complained about strewn toys again.

RESPECT THROUGH ENCOURAGEMENT

My husband has observed that everyone is "under-encouraged." When we step out of our front doors, the world seems to relish knocking us down. Sometimes our husbands feel they can't win. Work, family, even the church all have high expectations of our men's time and energy.

Many men related that words of encouragement from their wives translate into respect. They wanted their wives to understand the power of words. Many respondents desired for their wives to be more encouraging and less critical. I could almost feel their pain as I read their answers.

"I wish my wife understood that her words of encouragement do more for me than five times the criticism."

"I know my wife respects me when she says she's proud of me."

"I know my wife respects me when she accepts me for who I am and tells me, when she expresses her appreciation for me and the things that I do, and when she encourages and builds me up."

"I don't feel respected by my wife when she questions everything I do, or when she criticizes me in public."

Proverbs 16:24 says, "Pleasant words are a honeycomb, sweet to the soul and healing to the bones." We may forget that our husbands need our verbal encouragement. They never take it for granted.

Some wives may be at a loss because they were raised in homes without verbal affirmation. The following are a few simple phrases to help you begin to encourage your husband:

- Thank you.
- I appreciate it when you . . .
- I'm proud of you.
- I love you.
- I love being your wife.
- You handled that well.
- You're a great dad.
- You work so hard to provide for us.
- I'm glad I married you.

Two of the most underrated words in the English language are "thank you." We may feel we don't need to thank our husbands for taking out the trash, or putting the kids to bed, or mowing the lawn, or any other thing they do around the house. We see it as their jobs, their responsibilities, not worth our appreciation. But showing sincere gratitude builds our husbands.

Most men want their wife's approval more than any other

person's. Our husbands see themselves through our eyes. They long to be admired by the person who knows them the best.

Michael was a pastor for twenty years. Our last church, in the suburbs of Washington D.C., was filled with brilliant and powerful people. Each Sunday congressional staffers, White House personnel, attorneys, physicians, and even a few congressmen and senators sat in the pews. Yet every week Michael wanted to know what I thought of his sermon. The congregation was filled with people who were much smarter than I am; yet he valued my opinion most.

He was especially appreciative when I told him what his sermon meant to me, or how it changed my thinking or gave me a new perspective. The more specific I was in my encouragement, the more significantly he felt my words.

On the other hand, our criticism can cut our husbands to the core. We can discourage them from entering family life or even offering their help. In eternity it really won't matter if our husbands load the dishwasher just like we do or arrange the bed pillows the way we like.

THE IMPORTANCE OF TRUST

Our husbands equate respect with trust. They want to know that we trust their opinions, we trust their judgments, and we trust their decisions. Several men indicated that they felt respected when their wives asked for their input, especially on parenting issues. Others appreciated being trusted with decisions that their wives didn't agree with or fully comprehend.

Michael and I have very different parenting styles. I tend to have a more holistic approach, trying to understand our child's motivations for bad behavior. Michael tends to see things much more clearly. He sees behavior as black or white; I see it as gray. Because I spend more time with our children, I usually believe my perceptions are correct.

Michael will always listen to my insights, and will often agree that we should try my suggestions; however, at times he adamantly feels there is a better way to motivate or influence one of our children. I have learned through experience that when we disagree on our parenting choices, I am much wiser to follow his lead than to do it my way. In fact, when I have insisted on implementing my plan, it rarely works, and we end up going back to Michael's ideas anyway. As head of our home, God gives Michael wisdom and direction that I might not be privy to. When I voluntarily cooperate with my husband, I allow God to lead our family as He designed.

Our attitude in all this is paramount. If we follow our husbands' lead, but do so expecting him to fail, we rob him of our trust. No one makes the correct choice 100 percent of the time. If a husband knows his wife is just waiting for his decision to fail, he may abdicate his role of leadership, believing he is in a no-win situation. Respect means that I trust my husband's judgment and am willing to accept the outcome.

HE SAID . . . LEADING THE FAMILY IS HARD

My husband and I have a saying, "If I were king for a day . . ." followed with a change we'd make in a given situation. For instance, "If I were king for a day, our children would think cleaning their room was more fun than going to Disney World." We've discovered that being king is rarely all we expect it to be.

When it comes to leading our families, our husbands would overwhelmingly agree with this. Those who take their leadership seriously find it to be a daunting proposition as they feel the weight of their immense responsibility.

Our husbands pick up the mantle of leadership feeling ill equipped. As one gentleman wrote, "The Bible gives men the responsibility to lead the home, but I need a step-by-step manual." They are frustrated by their own sin and selfishness, and worry about how to lead their family spiritually. Our husbands are burdened by their own failures and concerned about the fallout of any unpopular decisions they make. They are also aware that their wives are intelligent, capable women, which causes them to question themselves when their decisions are met with resistance. No wonder many men allow their wives to assume the direction of the family.

John Maxwell once said, "If someone calls himself a leader, yet no one follows in his footsteps, then he's just out taking a walk!" As wives, we can empower our husbands' leadership by choosing to follow. We need to be sensitive to the difficulty of his role, especially when the family is experiencing life-altering choices. When we willingly submit, we are affirming our husband's manhood and agreeing to trust God's design for our marriage. As we take our husband's role seriously, he will too.

Man to Man

Chauvinists Need Not Apply

by Michael J. Easley

Husbands, love your wives, just as Christ loved the church and gave Himself up for her.

—*Ephesians 5:25 NASB*

HE WAS VISIBLY ANGRY. He was holding a large Bible, open to Ephesians chapter five. His nostrils flared and the veins in his neck pulsed as he asked me, "What version of the Bible do you read?"

"What version would you like me to read?" I replied.

"Well," he said, "I just want to know what version of the Bible you're reading because it says right here in mine, 'Wives, be submissive to your husbands!'"

His wife and another woman stood a few feet behind him. He was angry with me because I had just said, "Nowhere in Scripture does it say that a husband is to *tell* his wife to submit." After a few more harsh words, he stormed out of the marriage conference and did not return. His wife and the other woman—his sister-in-law, I was soon to learn—wept as he tore out of the room.

"It's not your fault," the sister-in-law said. "He has an anger problem." I spent the next thirty minutes listening to this poor woman and her sister recount the difficulty of living with this man.

A GOOD AND GODLY MAN

In this book, Cindy has tried to encourage your bride toward a biblical perspective on a subject most women find wholly disagreeable. Our wives are surrounded by voices that loathe the slightest suggestion that they should ever be submissive to anyone—much less us. But beyond your wife making a fundamental decision to obey the Lord and submit to Him and His Word, the next most significant piece of any wife being submissive to her husband is that her husband must be a good and godly man.

This has nothing to do with physical power, force of personality, or ability to yell louder than the next guy—which is why our friend from the conference had it all wrong. I am speaking of the innate character and quality of being a man. For the record, let there be no doubt, there is never a place for a man to *use* this power to harm his wife or family.

Yet I believe our culture has worked overtime to tame men, to feminize us. Our culture has systematically emasculated men and tried to domesticate us into some kind of warm, passive nonentity. *Sit there and watch this chick flick and enjoy it!*

I remember my dad never liked the cartoon strip *Blondie*. He observed that the hapless husband, Dagwood, was always the punch line of the joke, while wife, Blondie, was always right. Perhaps that's why I never cared for *Home Improvement* or *Everybody Loves Raymond* or other very successful sitcoms. Funny, yes, but funny at the expense of the husband.

But maybe we deserve it. Next time you are walking around in public, going to the grocery store, or in a place where you see couples together, just watch the men. Often we look like an uncomfortable appendage in a relationship. Maybe we're tired, bored, impatient, or sulking. Perhaps we're lagging behind or forging ahead. Perhaps we can see a little bit of the struggle because men have been like Agur: "Surely I am more stupid than any man, And I do not have the understanding of a man. Neither have I learned wisdom, Nor do I have the knowledge of the Holy One" (Proverbs 30:2–3 NASB).

H. L. Mencken, the famous critic (and cynic) of the early twentieth century, put it this way: "A man may be a fool and not know it, but not if he is married."

SEARCHING FOR ROLE MODELS

In our defense, we may be starting with a deficit. Maybe you had an extraordinary dad and he was a prince of a husband to your mom. But maybe you had a bad example. Maybe Dad was absent or abusive or an alcoholic. Maybe he screamed at Mom or hit her. Maybe he came home and threw back a six-pack before dinner. Maybe he was a jerk Monday through Saturday and put a suit on Sunday and smiled at his friends. Or maybe he was a pretty nice ol' guy who was a working stiff and never said much of anything.

So much of who we are is cast early in our experience. Even if we had good-to-great models of marriage and family, our wives probably had different experiences. Simply acknowledging that goes a long way. One of my mentors, Floyd Sharp, would often say, "It's not wrong, it's just different."

As I pass the fifty-year mark, I notice more and more how wonderfully my parents love each other. In their eighties, their relationship skills, while different than couples in our age bracket, are committed and effective. The sheer accumulation of their lives adds up to a rich texture of relationship. Their humor, patience, knowing smiles, and tender hugs reveal a life pretty well lived. Too often we hear negative comments about our parents' generation: I think they are remarkable people.

Fast-forward into a world of exponential divorce rates, single-parent homes, a shameless culture, and in the turn of a page it is hard to find any good and godly models. Even if you were blessed to have a positive example, the pressure from a broken culture never rests. You almost feel embarrassed to hold on to the belief that marriage was intended for one man to one woman for life.

To be a good and godly husband is an uphill trek on an unpaved road. To be the husband Christ wants you to be is a difficult journey and one in which you will be mocked, blamed, dismissed, accused, and find yourself feeling desperately alone at times. But to be the husband Christ wants you to be is a remarkable and holy goal. And it is otherworldly.

THE TRUTH ABOUT "MUTUAL SUBMISSION"

Solomon writes that "wisdom calls."[1] Wisdom is personified as shouting from the housetop, beckoning, "Come and get wisdom!" The prerequisite seems to be that we want it. Wisdom stands against pride, arrogance, evil, and the perverted. Biblical wisdom offers blessing. Simply put, wisdom is the application of knowledge. Scripture offers many examples, stories, narrative, and specific instruction about marriage. The best known—and least understood—are Paul's words to the Ephesians. Ephesians 5:25 may be one of the best-known verses about a husband's role in marriage, but too often we take it out of context.

Back up to Ephesians 5:21 (NASB), a generally stated principle: *"and be subject to one another in the fear of Christ."* Some argue that this means "mutual submission." This idea is that there is no real or *final* leadership, but the husband and wife have equal value, equal roles, and equal say. Proponents of "mutual submission" argue that this means both wives and husbands are to compromise and acquiesce to one another. But a straightforward and careful study of the context demonstrates it cannot mean a mutual submission. In every leadership relationship, submission to a leader is involved. The apostle Paul articulates several "leadership-submission" relationships: wives to husbands, children to parents, slaves to masters.[2]

In other words, the concept of submission means submission *to someone in authority.* Ephesians 5:22 (NASB), *"Wives be subject to your own husbands,* **as to the Lord***"* clearly cannot mean "mutual submission." Christ does not acquiesce to us. Christ does not sit down and talk with us and compromise and *submit* to our ideas. Submission to Christ means submission to His authority.[3]

YOU HUSBANDS, LOVE YOUR WIVES!

But then: *"Husbands, love your wives, just as Christ also loved the church"* (Eph. 5:25a NASB).

It is no surprise that the verbal form *love* in this passage is an imperative, a command. That means we might render it: *You husbands, love your wives!* Envision a drill sergeant giving you an order. But the passage doesn't bark orders at us; the Word of God compels us to love *just as Christ also loved the church.* Men, this is not merely a command to go and love your bride but to love her in the same manner that Christ loved His church: *to give Himself up for her.*

This love is different from anything we expect. It knocks over our categories and definitions of love. It comes as a surprise as we study through the Savior's love for sinners. This kind of love is very rarely understood because we hardly ever see it in our experience. "Love" is usually characterized as an infatuation, a head-spinning emotion, or reduced to sexual attraction. When love is seen these ways, it is a distortion.

The Bible, however, paints a different picture. Consider:

- Love gives to another. (1 Corinthians 13:5)
- Love places others' needs ahead of your own. (Ephesians 4:2; Philippians 2:3)
- Love cares for and nourishes another person. (Romans 12:10; Ephesians 5:29)
- Love is not predicated upon a person's response. (Romans 5:8; Colossians 3:19)
- Love sacrifices. (John 15:13; Ephesians 5:2, 25; Hebrews 10:12; 1 Peter 3:7)
- Love obeys. (John 8:29; 13:34–35; 14:15, 24)

This is how Christ loved His church. It is a love compelled by a greater love, a love to obey the Father. Every time I read Ephesians 5:25 (NASB), I am struck by the phrase "and gave Himself up for her." How can a husband read that verse and then turn around and demand submission from his wife?

When Christ surrendered Himself to arrest, trial, mocking, restraint, crucifixion, all at the hands of sinners, He did not hang on the cross and insult His evil captors. Christ *gave Himself up for her.* He did not blame His disciples. He did not cry out to the Father to judge the church, to destroy those who wanted to kill Him. He submitted to His Father's will and asked the Father to forgive those who wanted Him dead. How could Jesus Christ do this? Why didn't He call on ten thousand angels to annihilate Pilate, the Roman guard, the leaders who wanted Him murdered by inhumane torture? How in the world did He *submit* to this? Because He loved the Father and He loved you and me.

Husbands, love your wives, just as Christ also loved the church, and gave Himself up for her (NASB).

This does not mean that love is without emotion. Wonderful feelings can and do accompany love. But the primary motivation for this love is far different from the kinds of feelings we think are supposed to be love.

Chauvinists need not apply.

Sacrificial love puts the needs of others first. Dying to self isn't hard, it's near impossible. To look God in the eye and say, "I want to love my wife like Christ loved You: that is my goal as a husband."

Parenting four kids has proved to be the best and hardest

job in my life. I know of no other task so demanding, so rewarding, so overwhelming. As parents, we generally know what is best for our kids. When they are very young, we protect them from burns, hurts, and toddling into traffic. We use child guards to keep them from getting into the cabinets where chemicals reside, from getting into drawers where sharp objects might lurk, and to cover up electrical outlets. We know these things will hurt a child. As they get into their twos and threes, we watch them test things more and more. While we wish they'd run to obey, they seem to run to disobey. They see what they can get away with. They push the edge, eye the prize, and try to cheat their way to some "reward" by not obeying.

But we know that brushing your teeth, getting good rest, eating your vegetables, and doing your homework is the path of good. These things are important and we expect our kids to obey because we're the all-knowing parent. I wonder if our dear Father longs for us to *run to obey*, to trust, to "eat our spiritual vegetables," knowing what is good for us.

TAKING INITIATIVE

Countless books and articles are churned out diagnosing and prescribing how leadership works. Within the context of a marriage, the husband is to be loving in his leadership. But how does this work in practice? Perhaps the best way to think about it is taking initiative.

Initiative is taking the first step. It is beginning. It is introducing something to start the process.

When Cindy and I were dating, we would go out to eat once a week. We didn't have much money so it was a given we went somewhere cheap. I vividly remember asking her, "Where would you like to go out to eat?" She always deferred. She'd always say, "I don't care." Soon into our marriage, the simple act of choosing where to go out to eat became a conflict. I'd ask, "Where would you like to go?" and she'd respond with the predictable "I don't care—where do you want to go?" This would turn into an argument. It seemed to me she had something in mind but wouldn't tell me for fear I wouldn't like it. Or perhaps she didn't want to go or didn't want to spend the money but wouldn't say it. So this silly conflict got bigger and bigger. So, I determined to give her choices. I'd ask, "OK, would you like Chinese, Italian, or Mexican?" To which she replied, "I don't care, which would you choose?"

Then I notched it up higher and asked, "OK, if you were going out without me and could choose, where would you go?" All along, I thought I was doing her a favor by giving her options—but she genuinely did not care. For Cindy, it was more important that I took time to plan and that we were out on a date. The place didn't matter. For me, I was becoming stressed from trying to please my wife and trying to figure out how to get her to tell me what she wanted.

This seemingly trivial issue required a number of candid

discussions. I was frustrated that she couldn't make a decision, and she was frustrated because she genuinely did not care and was wanting me to choose.

Today, I ask, "Would you like to go try that new Mexican restaurant?" She might offer, "No, I don't want to eat that much food—how about that salad place?" The underlying issue became, how am I as a loving leader going to sort through this so that we have a great time together?

In our relationship, this scenario plays out consistently. From going on a date, inviting couples over for dinner, to choosing a church, to buying a car, a house, you name it. In our marriage relationship, Cindy prefers that I take the initiative. That does not mean I do everything or plan everything. In our case, she likes planning some things. But in the main, it communicates love to her when I take the initiative.

For years, I've taken Cindy on a lunch date every week. We have seasons where it's hard to manage, but for the most part, we have a lunch date each week. For us it is a relational barometer. We talk about everything. We talk about the kids, budgets, work, goals, plans, dreams, vacations, and house projects we want to do. We talk a lot about our schedules. Just managing all the things going on in the average week takes tons of communication. Cindy and I joke that the key to our marriage has been "Wednesday lunches." And I cannot tell you how many hundreds of men ask me, "Now, what do you *do* when you take her out to lunch?"

The irony of it all is that I totally understand. For many men, spending that much time with their wife might feel intimidating. The reason? Because we are out of step and out of sync with our relationship. Just start. Begin. Pursue her. And don't worry if you don't have profound conversations every time. Just keep taking her out on dates. And a little free advice: go to movies or invite other couples only as rare exceptions. I have nothing against movies or friends—we have some fantastic couple friends—I just know that you don't have a conversation at the movies, and usually you don't develop the skills for your marriage. You probably won't end up talking about your relationship.

Take the initiative to pursue your wife all of your life. Never stop.

Most importantly, as you take initiative in different areas, it folds into your spiritual relationship.

Years ago, Dennis Rainey challenged me to pray with Cindy every day. At that time I rarely prayed with Cindy. Sure, we'd say "grace" over a meal, but as far as holding-hands-closing-eyes-and-praying stuff, no way. For some reason I'd rather sign up for military service, go climb a cliff, or hang glide. But pray with my wife? It scared me stiff. The main reason it scared me was that I had not done it in so long, to ask her to pray would be a stark admission of my failure in this area. Plus, she might have a heart attack.

I still remember the first night I asked her. We were going to bed and had our little requisite good night kiss. Scared to death, I reached over my left hand and asked, "Do you want to pray?" And you know what she said? She said, "Sure!" Then she prayed and then I prayed. I lived.

That has been about twenty years ago now. Every night when we go to bed (unless we go to bed at different times), we pray together. And I am the one who still asks, every night. I plop my hand over onto her side of the bed and say, "Let's pray." And she always does. Well, once in a while she might say, "Why don't you just pray . . . I'm too tired." And so I do.

Initiative. Taking the first step. Asking the first question. Lovingly leading. Here are some suggestions.

Can we read this book together?

Can I show you something I'm learning in the Scripture?

Let's pray about this right now!

How about we invite so-and-so for dinner?

Would you be interested in being in a small group?

What would you think about joining a Bible study?

How about pursuing that older couple?

Let's go to a marriage conference!

What goals would you like to set for us as a family?

How can you and I serve God as a couple?

STUDY YOUR WIFE

"When a girl marries, she exchanges the attentions of many men for the inattention of one."

—HELEN ROWLAND

In graduate school I had a professor who constantly reminded us, "Men, be a student of your wife." In God's great kindness, I've been trying to study Cindy for over twenty-seven years. I study her mood and her interests. I study what makes her smile, laugh, and cry. I study what makes her light up, what makes her angry. I study what gives her rest, joy, and what lightens her load. I study her all the time and I still can't figure her out. So I keep on studying.

One day I was complaining to my mentor Floyd Sharp about Cindy. I don't remember what it was, but I was whining to him about my troubles. He listened intently and then he said, "Not the same thing . . . [he said that all the time]. But Deborah and I have been married thirty-eight years and I still can't figure her out." Then he looked away into the air and said, "Deborah is an enigma to me." I still laugh when I think about it.

Floyd was telling me—and you—you can't figure her out. You will never understand her. But you keep on studying.

First Peter 3:7 (NASB) begins, "You husbands in the same way, live with your wives in an understanding way." Note the passage does not say, "Understand your wife." The literal reading of the verse would be something like, *Husbands, live together according to knowledge.* In other words, I think the implication is, try to know her, try to understand her, study her.

Then the passage moves into a controversial phrase: "You

husbands in the same way, live with your wives in an understanding way, as with someone *weaker*, since she is a woman; and show her honor as a fellow heir of the grace of life, so that your prayers will not be hindered."

I would urge you not to rush over to your bride and say, "Honey, did you know you are weaker?"

But seriously, look at it a little closer. Weaker is used in Scripture of Paul's physical appearance (2 Corinthians 10:10); the disciples being unable to stay awake and pray for a little while (Matthew 26:41); to draw a contrast that the *weakness of God is stronger than men* (1 Corinthians 1:25), and that some have weak consciences and they worry about things that a "stronger" person does not worry about (1 Corinthians 8:7–9). The point is that women have a different capacity than men.

This does not mean women are inferior or less able than men. It does not mean that women are not strong. It does not mean women are not as smart or emotionally strong. (It is no secret that Cindy is a lot smarter than me in many areas.) Some argue that the passage merely states that women are physically weaker than men. Any husband knows, wives are extremely strong in many ways. But it does tell me that Cindy's capacity is different from mine.

Nancy Groom writes, "It is significant that Peter (1 Peter 3:7) forbids any inferiority-superiority spiritual distinctions between men and women (they are equally heirs), while at the same time he insists on the authority-submission functional distinction in marriage (submit and be considerate). Husbands and wives are equal inheritors of God's wonderful grace through Jesus, but they are called to live out their redemption by observing their differing marital responsibilities as leaders and responders."[4]

Context, as we've already seen, is critical. As we continue the verse, we read that the "weakness" point has *nothing to do* with this being a negative indictment; it has to do with the importance of treating her with *honor as a fellow heir of the grace of life, so that your prayers will not be hindered.* Or, said another way: Husband, treat your wife with extraordinary care because she is a fellow heir . . . and this is your role as a loving leader. A good and godly husband understands that his wife is a coheir to the kingdom of God. A good and godly husband understands that the same grace that saved his wife saved him and he is on equal footing when it comes to salvation.

Last, the passage ends with a note on prayer. In some way—and I admit I don't fully understand—the way I treat Cindy impacts my prayer life. If we live out-of-sorts with our wives, if we treat them disrespectfully, if we don't care for them as a treasure, it will adversely affect our prayers. If we don't honor our wives the way God intended, why would He honor our prayer requests?

Try to study your wife a little more.

BEING THE HUSBAND GOD WANTS YOU TO BE

"A man, after he has brushed off the dust and chips of his life, will have left only the hard, clean question: Was it good or was it evil? Have I done well—or ill?"

—JOHN STEINBECK[5]

So how does a man love his wife as Christ loved the church? Answer: you die for her. You don't blame her or tell her to submit. You don't lord leadership over her. You don't sit and bark orders or play the trump card. You don't disengage and wait for her. You get up off the sofa of life and become involved in your marriage.

Being a loving leader is a tough assignment. To love your wife as Christ loves the church is for me a lifelong project. At times I'm grouchy, selfish, peevish, angry, sullen, and can sit and stew in my juices. I can hide in my computer always doing work. I can cozy up to the TV and watch news for hours. Or, I can pursue my precious bride.

I often wonder, when couples have struggles and drift apart, what was it that brought them together in the first place? What was that attraction, that gleam, that infatuation? What pulled you together like two magnets? And where did it go?

We live in a world that will never help you become the

man God wants you to be. We are surrounded by failed marriages, failed morality, failed finances, and disposable lives. But the God of the universe longs for our marriages to glorify Him. My marriage is not merely about me and not even about Cindy and me. Our marriage is about two very imperfect sinners being glued together to somehow give glory to His name.

A loving leader, a good and godly husband, sets aside the injustices. He puts on his armor and deflects the little jabs and jolts that are distractions. He suits up. And he gets back in the game over and over and over again. He makes a fundamental decision: I will try—with God's Holy Spirit's help—to be the husband and father He wants me to be. I will run after it harder than my career. I will run after it harder than money. And when I fail—and I will—I will promptly ask forgiveness and get back in the game. But it's no mere game, it is life.

Too many men quit. They stop. They get sidelined. I read once that success is simply doing the things others don't want to do. Here are some you can do—any man can do—and it will make a difference in your loving leadership to be the good and godly husband He wants you to be.

And here's the prize. You and your marriage will represent the Sovereign King of the universe. He died to set you free and He will use your marriage to make a difference in the lives in your home and around the world.

NOTES

1. Proverbs 8 also offers that wisdom is available to anyone who asks.

2. Neither the New Testament nor Paul sanctions slavery. In some situations, indentured servitude was a volitional relationship where an impoverished person became a person's servant. The spoils of war also resulted in the acquisition of servant-slaves. The biblical injunction is not arguing *for* slavery but acknowledging it did exist. In those situations, there was a proper "leadership-submission" response. The New Testament gave more freedom to women and slaves than perhaps any other religion or societal system.

3. For extensive reading regarding the roles of men and women, visit http://www.cbmw.org/. Additionally, *Recovering Biblical Manhood and Womanhood,* John Piper and Wayne Grudem, eds. (Wheaton, Ill.: Good News Publishers, 2006) is an exceptional resource for further study.

4. Nancy Groom, *Married without Masks* (Colorado Springs: NavPress, 1996), 169.

5. American author John Steinbeck (1902–1968), cited in the *Dallas Morning News*, November 22, 1993.

12

Frequently Asked Questions

But the goal of our instruction is love from a pure heart and a good conscience and a sincere faith.

—*1 Timothy 1:5 NASB*

1. HOW IS SUBMISSION different than just giving in? Sometimes it may feel exactly the same. However, the difference is in my communication and respect. I have clearly stated my opinion and listened to Michael's as well. I have assisted him by gathering all the facts he needs to make a wise assessment. Rather than "giving in" to him, I am freeing him to accept the weight of the decision. My attitude is the key to reflecting my respect for his leadership. If I willingly and cheerfully follow his leadership, I act in godly submission. If I sulk or pout, I am compromising, or giving in, and grudgingly following his headship.

2. Should you submit in all things, or are there exceptions?

Submission does not mean that we follow a husband blindly. Submission never condones allowing your husband to violate you or to break the law. A wife should never follow her husband's leadership if it would cause her to break moral principles or the laws of the government. For example, submission is not an excuse for polygamy, illegal activity, or abortion.

A woman in an abusive relationship should seek help immediately. Headship never gives a husband the right to harm his wife or children, either physically or emotionally. If you are in this kind of marriage, I would encourage you to seek counseling from a pastor, close friend, family, or legal authorities. In the case of abuse, a wife should remove herself from the situation in hopes of getting her husband the help he needs. Intervening when our husbands are trapped in destructive behavior is not only right but is also the duty of a wife as a helpmate.

3. What do you do when you are convinced God "told" you one thing and your husband is convinced He said something else?

The expression "God told me" usually causes me to pause and ask specific questions. First, how did you hear from God? We often "feel" a certain way and decide it is of God. Perhaps we look at the circumstances leading to a decision and conclude it must be of God. However, God's Word must always take precedence over our experience. God will never "tell" us to do something that is contrary to His written Word.

Next, we must look at the principles in God's Word as we make decisions. One principle is to seek the wisdom of godly counselors. If you and your husband have sought for an answer through God's Word and the counsel of godly people and still disagree, then your role is to follow his leadership.

This is the definition of submission: voluntarily placing yourself under your husband's leadership even when you do not agree with it. In my view, submission is not at issue when we *agree* with our husband's direction. Godly submission is seen in our humility and in our readiness to yield for the higher purpose of allowing our husbands to lead. God is sovereign, even when our husbands lead in ways that we don't like. Remember that a wife's submission is ultimately to God, not man.

4. Are there ever times a wife doesn't have to submit, like when she is staying at home with the kids and he is at work all day?

In a complementarian home, a wife is always under her husband's headship, even when he is not present in the home. That said, he should trust her to make decisions concerning the home and children even when he is not available. It's not good parenting to use the old phrase, "Wait until your father gets home."

In our home, Michael and I are a team. Our children know that when I speak, I speak for both of us, and vice versa. When situations arise that I need to discuss with him, I simply explain that to our children. I've found that Michael will often have insights into an issue or a child that are different from my own. When we work this out together, we have a better chance of successfully parenting.

On the other hand, at times Michael and I disagree on a parenting technique. In that case I certainly voice my opinion; however, in the end I believe that Michael will be the one standing before God as ultimately responsible for our family.

Communication is the key to building a united front in parenting. When Michael and I exchange our ideas and find a shared understanding of child rearing, we usually will act in tandem. However, when I undermine Michael's authority in the home by allowing something he disapproves of, I abdicate my role as a helpmate.

For example, my husband does not want our children to own a gaming system. Although I agree with his reasoning, at times I want to give in to their pleas. If I get them a Nintendo or Xbox, I am discouraging Michael's leadership by making his headship less important than our kids' desires. In doing so, I not only show disrespect for Michael's authority in our home, but I teach my children to do the same.

5. **What do you do about a husband who tells his wife she needs to submit?**

For several years Michael and I spoke with FamilyLife Weekend to Remember Conferences. One session of the weekend was aimed directly at husbands and their roles as loving leaders. During that session Michael would often explain to the men that the Bible never gives permission for a husband to tell his wife to submit. Occasionally, this concept would confuse and upset someone in the audience.

Yes, the Bible does define the roles of head/helper and loving leader/submissive wife. However, these roles are never ours to demand from our spouse. These roles are given to create harmony in our home and as a physical image of Christ's relationship to the church. Obviously, if our husbands love us sacrificially, like Christ loved the church, our role of submission is much easier. In the same way, if we are yielding ourselves in godly submission to our husband's leadership, we would be easier to love.

If a husband is saying, "Submit to me," he is obviously frustrated in his leadership. If a wife hears these words from her husband, I would encourage her to gently explain to him what he could do to make his leadership easier to follow. We can do this without demanding but by explaining our needs in a way that he can understand. A woman's attitude of respect is the key to effective communication. Her desire to follow must be clear to her husband so he does not feel threatened.

I would also encourage the wife to look closely at her own heart. Is she being stubborn and unwilling to follow because she disagrees with her husband? Is she fearful of the future? Does she lack confidence in her husband's leadership? Is she simply a controller who needs to hold on to the power of the family to feel safe? In the end, a woman's trust in God determines her willingness to yield to her husband's authority.

6. Does submitting to my husband mean he can do anything he wants and I have to live with it?

Submission never means remaining silent when you are concerned about your husband's behavior. Sometimes women do not express their thoughts or feelings because they fear they will rock the status quo. Many of us are natural pleasers. We want our husbands to be happy with us, so we don't adequately express ourselves. Unfortunately, this sends mixed messages to the men in our lives. Unless we clearly express frustration or disappointment, they assume we are fine with their actions. The key to our expression is that we communicate our feelings with respect.

Often this question arises in reference to a man's hobbies that take him away from the family. Most men and women work long hours during the week and may have differing expectations about how free time should be spent. You may think you and your husband should spend time with the kids, while your husband may want to spend the weekend on the golf course with his friends.

Voice your concerns and your needs. Be specific. Keep your tone calm and your words nonthreatening. Try to make a plan that can accommodate both of you. Many men (and women) need the stress relief that a hobby can bring. For years my husband played racquetball several times each week. At times, I was resentful that he didn't rush home to relieve me of child rearing, yet I knew that hitting that little ball at the four walls would release enough endorphins to bring him home in a more relaxed mood. If I didn't nag or whine when he arrived home, Michael was usually more than happy to take a crabby child or sweep the floor *as long as I honestly, and respectfully, explained how I felt and asked for his help.*

Sometimes we want our husbands to know how we feel without having to explain ourselves. This is unfair. As Michael likes to say, "Honey, after twenty-seven years of marriage I still can't read your mind."

7. How do you follow a husband who doesn't know where he wants to go? How do you live with that instability?

It's hard to follow someone who doesn't know his own path. This reminds me of Sarah, Abraham's wife. Abraham received direction from God to go, yet God did not tell him where. Hebrews 11:8 explains, "Abraham, when called to go to a place he would later receive as his inheritance, obeyed and went, even though he did not know where he was going."

Abraham followed God's voice. Sarah followed Abraham. Perhaps she wondered if Abe heard God correctly. She packed up all of their belongings and headed to an unknown destination.

As women, we have a need for stability. We want to know where we will be next week, next year, and five years from now. We want to plan and nest and know we will have the security of a settled life. Sometimes this is not to be.

I've found that God can use the instability of my circumstances to remind me that He is my security. When I want to cling to my worldly surroundings, God will upset my balance so that I will cling only to Him.

Your husband may know the direction he is headed but hasn't adequately communicated that to you. Take a weekend away without kids and spend time together. Discuss your present and your future. Dream. Hash out ideas. Give your husband your insights on his gifts and abilities, helping him work through his own insecurities. Even if your husband doesn't have a detailed life plan, you will probably feel more secure simply knowing his thought processes.

Years ago Michael was being pursued for a position in California. The leadership of the church was enamored with him, and he was equally captivated with their enthusiasm. As I watched this unfold, I realized that my husband was being swayed by personalities instead of by the opportunities for ministry. When I expressed my concerns, Michael agreed. It was hard for him to turn down the offer, but he realized my insights kept him from making a decision he would later regret. Three more years passed before we had a clear direction on where to go. The in-between time was hard, but it gave us the opportunity to seek God's direction together.

8. Does submission mean I have to agree with everything my husband believes?

Submission does not mean checking your brain at the door of your home. While it is important to share the fundamentals of faith with your husband, it is perfectly reasonable for you to disagree on the finer points of theology. Godly men and women, scholars, have differing views of certain areas of Scripture. God inspired all Scripture, but not all Scripture is black-and-white. In the gray matters, you can each hold to your own views, as long as you do so with respect. If an area continues to be a source of conflict, consider making it off-limits for discussion. If this subject becomes a topic of conversation in public, I would encourage you to keep silent out of respect for your husband, *especially if he feels threatened by your disagreement.*

Remember, submission is humility. When we let go of our pride, we are able to place our husbands' needs above our own.

9. **What do you do when your husband is about to make a bad decision that will hurt others?**

Begin by explaining your concern. Your husband may not see how his decision will affect those around him. However, he may be well aware of the repercussions and still believe it is the right thing to do.

Sometimes leaders make unpopular decisions. As women, we may perceive the emotions of everyone around us. We don't want anyone to have hurt feelings. Good leadership will consider those feelings, but we can't avoid a decision based solely on those feelings.

Part of leadership is on-the-job training. Managers learn to make good decisions by making lots of them, including some that are doomed for failure. As wives, we need to step back and give our husbands the freedom to learn, both from their successes and failures.

Sometimes we don't want our husbands to do things that affect others because we are concerned with how it will affect their reputations. We want everyone to like them . . . and us. My husband often makes very hard decisions. I know he will be criticized and misunderstood. Although I would love to wipe those decisions away, he is responsible to do what he believes to be right. The best I can do is support him in his choices even if they would not have been my choices.

10. How do you submissively disagree?

Respectfully. With well-chosen words, a calm voice, without blame or accusation. In marriage, it's important to learn to fight fair. I don't really mean to "fight" in the raised voice, temper tantrum sort of way. I do mean we need to be able to air our differences reasonably.

Stick to the facts, be kind in your word choice, and listen to your husband's side of the argument just as you want to be listened to. Look past the words to the hidden meanings. Repeat what you hear your husband saying so you can make sure you understand correctly, and ask him to do the same with you. The goal is to agree. If you cannot agree on a subject, then aim to understand each other. It's fine to "agree to disagree" about an issue as long as you both can leave it that way without further antagonism.

At times Michael and I will disagree, and he will acquiesce to my way of thinking. That is perfectly within his right as the head of our home. If he does not, it is my role to remain respectful of his leadership even in those areas in which we cannot see eye-to-eye.

11. What "roles" do we assume and who does what in the home? For example, in finances, housekeeping, etc.

We often have certain expectations about who will be responsible for certain household chores. We might even mentally categorize tasks by gender, thinking, "That's a man's job" or "That's a woman's job." Contrary to orthodox thought, the person who takes out the garbage and mows the lawn is not automatically assigned to the head or helper in the relationship. Rather, it is a result of personal choice, ability, and availability to complete that task.

When Michael and I married, we both assumed certain duties based on what our parents had done. He would balance the checkbook, I would take out the trash, etc. Over time, we learned that he was actually more domestic than I am, and I enjoy keeping track of our spending. Because of Michael's time restraints, I still do most of the cooking and cleaning. But because he is a perfectionist, he is better at both of those things than I am. As a result, he almost always prepares at least part of the meal when we have company.

I have started working more on the lawn, *because I love to do it*. Once Michael realized I could handle the mower without mauling our flower beds, he was willing to relinquish this job to me. My helping in this way gave him more time to do the detail work in our yard, like trimming bushes and clearing out weeds.

Some homes divide the workload into inside/outside labor. Others may choose to have a chore chart, or take turns in doing specific duties. One may cook dinner, while the other cleans up afterward. Setting this example of teamwork is important as you establish a pattern in your home for your children to follow.

A complementarian marriage does not mean having

specific, programmed duties. The head/helper relationship is revealed in our attitudes concerning home leadership. This is much higher level thinking than having designated tasks.

12. Does the role of husband and wife (head/helper) play out in the body of Christ?

Entire books have been written to answer this question, which is really, "What is the role of women in the church?"

First, I believe that women have far more significance and a greater role in the church than they have limitations. However, I would argue that the disciples who established the New Testament church placed two specific limitations on women. The first is that the office of elder seems limited to men. Titus 1:6 specifically states that, "An elder must be blameless, the husband of but one wife, a man whose children believe and are not open to the charge of being wild and disobedient."

Romans 16:1 lists a woman, Phoebe, as a servant or deaconess of the church, but there is no record of a woman as an elder. Although some women, and men, would argue that this limitation is a product of that culture, I would prefer to err on the side of literal interpretation of these words.

The second restriction is in the area of women teaching men the Word of God. Paul wrote to Timothy, "But I do not allow a woman to teach or exercise authority over a man, but to remain quiet" (1 Tim. 2:12 NASB)

Women do not seem to be constrained to teach anything

but the Scripture to men. That would allow women to teach in all other areas, as well as read Scripture, lead worship, or serve in any other capacity as long as she is not exercising authority over men in the congregation. Jesus, and His disciples, including Paul, elevated the value of women far above that culture, noting their contributions to the ministry.

Today, I've observed that women may be their own worst enemy when it comes to their contributions to the local church. Women usually find the freedom, even the encouragement, to get involved in every area of church life. However, when a woman becomes obsessed with a title (i.e., elder or pastor), she reveals her need for power and authority more than her desire to serve. Effective ministry is service, and requires humility of anyone who desires to be in leadership. Christ is our ultimate example:

> *Your attitude should be the same as that of Christ Jesus: who, being in very nature[1] God, did not consider equality with God something to be grasped, but made himself nothing, taking the very nature[2] of a servant, being made in human likeness. And being found in appearance as a man, he humbled himself and became obedient to death—even death on a cross! (Phil. 2:5–8)*

NOTES
1. Or *in the form of.*
2. Or *the form.*

Epilogue
The Proverbs 31 Woman

The Example of Ruth Graham

Her children rise up and bless her; her husband also, and he praises her, saying: "Many daughters have done nobly, but you excel them all."

—*Proverbs 31:28–29 NASB*

RUTH BELL GRAHAM died on Thursday, June 14, 2007. That evening her obituary appeared in my email in-box, sent to me from *Christianity Today*. Reading the article, I thought, *That's it! Ruth Graham is the embodiment of a helpmate to her husband. She is the Proverbs 31 woman.*

As you can read for yourself, Ruth Graham was spunky, intelligent, capable, and wise. She chose to elevate her husband's dreams above her own, certainly surrendering parts of herself along the way. But I bet if Ruth were here today, she would tell us that she gained far more than she sacrificed. That's how submission often works. When we choose to use our vast resources to further our husbands' leadership and success, we are the ones who gain the most.

RUTH GRAHAM DIES AT 87

Billy Graham's wife of nearly 64 years was a distinguished communicator of God's power and peace in her own right.

Marshall Shelley

Ruth Bell Graham, wife of evangelist Billy Graham, died Thursday at her home at Little Piney Cove in Montreat, North Carolina. She was 87.

She was born to missionary parents in Tsingkiang, China, in 1920, where she was raised in staunch Presbyterian piety, with daily doses of private and family devotions and being expected to memorize large portions of the Bible. Her high school years were spent in a boarding school in Pyongyang (now North Korea).

In 1940, at Wheaton College in Illinois, she met a classmate who invited her to a performance of Handel's *Messiah*. From that first date, the relationship between Ruth Bell and Billy Graham took off. Before they parted for the summer of 1941, Billy asked Ruth to marry him. She didn't say yes immediately, but within a few weeks, she wrote him to say that she believed their relationship was "of the Lord."

They graduated from Wheaton in June 1943 and were married on Friday, August 13. Returning from their honeymoon, Ruth fell sick, but instead of calling to cancel his preaching engagement in Ohio to stay by her bedside, Billy checked Ruth into a hospital and kept the speaking appointment, sending her a telegram and a box of candy.

So began her adjustment to her husband's intense calling to preach, which meant extended times of separation. Yet "I'd rather have Bill part-time," she often said, "than anybody else full-time."

Ruth was a student of the Bible. "She knows the Bible a lot better than I do," Billy was quick to admit. And she provided a measure of grit that complemented Billy's more diplomatic style.

When Billy warmly recalled his meeting with the president of Mexico—"He even embraced me"—Ruth quickly added, "Oh, Bill, don't be flattered. He did that to Castro, too."

Yet she never tried to place herself in the spotlight: "That's not my wad of gum."

Much of her ministry was with her 5 children, 19 grandchildren, and more than a dozen great-grandchildren. She personally selected and purchased 150 heavily wooded acres near Black Mountain, North Carolina, where she designed the "mountain primitive" house that became their home.

Ruth authored several books, including *One Wintry Night*, a collection of her poetry, and *Prodigals and Those Who Love Them*, which draw on her experience as a mother of two "spiritual wanderers" to encourage others whose loved ones strayed from the faith.

Her ministry also took other forms. After inheriting a tidy

sum from her father's estate, she gave it all away, mostly to an orphanage in Mexico. She also cared for female prisoners, including Velma Barfield, a North Carolina woman who made a commitment to Christ while on death row before her execution for murder. Ruth was also a driving force in creating the Ruth and Billy Graham Children's Health Center at Memorial Mission Hospital in Asheville, North Carolina.

In 1988, thanks to Ruth's efforts, the Grahams went on a 17-day trip through China, where she was greeted as "a daughter of China" and Billy as "a man of peace." Both of them were received by Premier Li Peng.

On May 2, 1996, Billy and Ruth Graham received the Congressional Gold Medal, the highest honor Congress can bestow upon a citizen, in the Rotunda of the U.S. Capitol in Washington, D.C.

In his remarks, Senate Majority Leader Bob Dole said, "When the idea of awarding a Congressional Gold Medal to Dr. Graham was first raised, it received something rare in this building—unanimous approval. So too did the idea of honoring Ruth Graham, Billy's remarkable partner of 53 years and a distinguished communicator of God's power and peace in her own right."

Ruth was known for being a woman of grace but also of outspoken forthrightness and wit.

When asked if she and her husband always agreed on

everything, she said, "My goodness, no! If we did, there would be no need for one of us!"

When Ruth answered the phone one day, the caller asked, "Is Billy handy?" She retorted, "Not very. But he keeps trying."

In 1952, Billy briefly entertained the possibility of running for President. Ruth quickly quashed that notion by calling him to say: "I don't think the American people would vote for a divorced president, and if you leave ministry for politics, you will certainly have a divorce on your hands."

Billy once described the secret of their more than 60-year marriage: "Ruth and I are happily incompatible."

Perhaps the best assessment of her contributions, however, came from the late T. W. Wilson, a boyhood friend of Billy's who became a trusted member of his evangelistic team.

"There would have been no Billy Graham as we know him today had it not been for Ruth," he said. "They have been a great team."

Appendix 1
For Further Consideration

Chapter 1

1. Read Genesis, chapters 1–2.
   a. What was the only thing in creation that God said was not good? Why?
   b. Why do you think God created the woman in a different way than He created Adam?
2. Read John 14:16–17.
   a. Who is the helper mentioned here?
   b. What is the role of the Holy Spirit in our lives? (In this passage the word "helper" means "comforter, advocate, intercessor.")
   c. How can we be this kind of helper to our husbands?

3. Read Ephesians 5:22–33.
   a. What distinct role did God give the wife? The husband?
   b. What is the mystery Paul refers to in verse 32?
   c. In verse 33, how does the admonition for a wife to respect her husband relate to her role in marriage?

Chapter 2

1. Read Genesis 3:1–7.
   a. How did the Serpent convince Eve to eat the forbidden fruit?
   b. How was Adam complicit in this sin? What should he have done?
   c. What was the immediate result of their sin?
2. Read Genesis 3:8–13.
   a. How was Adam and Eve's relationship altered with God?
   b. Whom did Adam blame for his sin?
   c. Whom did Eve blame for her sin?
3. Read Genesis 3:14–21.
   a. What was God's curse on the Serpent?
   b. What was the consequence of disobedience for the woman?
   c. What was the consequence for Adam?
   d. In Genesis 3:21, what final act was taken to "cover" the sin of Adam and Eve?

Chapter 3

1. Read 1 Peter 3:1–6.
    a. What attributes of a wife will be more likely to win her husband to Christ?
    b. Why does Peter caution women against only focusing on external adornments?
    c. What attitude did Sarah have toward Abraham that we should emulate?
2. Read Philippians 2:14–15.
    a. What do you most frequently complain about?
    b. What does complaining communicate to God? To your husband?
    c. How can you be a light in your home? Be specific.
3. Read Proverbs 31:10–12.
    a. What do you do to gain the trust of your husband?
    b. How are you an asset to your husband in your home?
    c. How do you enhance your husband's reputation in your community? (i.e., with neighbors, his coworkers, friends, etc.)

Chapter 4

1. Read James 1:2–4.
    a. Why does God allow us to face trials in our marriages?
    b. How do difficult situations in marriage cause us to grow in our faith?

    c. What is the end result of our perseverance while facing hard times? (See also James 1:12.)

2. Read Philippians 4:11–13.

    a. Think of the "other" words in your marriage ceremony: worse, poorer, sickness. How can you remain content in even these difficult circumstances?

    b. What is the "secret" to contentment?

    c. In the context it is written, what does "I can do everything through [Christ]" mean?

3. Read Galatians 6:2.

    a. Our husbands can have many burdens, from health issues to job loss. What are some of the pressures your husband is facing?

    b. What are you currently doing that might add to his load?

    c. What can you do that would offer your husband some relief from his burdens?

Chapter 5

1. Read James 3:1–12.

    a. What are the five images used to describe the power of our words? Explain them.

    b. How does what we say truly represent who we are?

    c. What are the positive and negative aspects of our words?

2. Read Ephesians 4:29–32.
   a. Define "unwholesome" words.
   b. How can what we say grieve the Holy Spirit?
   c. What attitudes and language are we to stop?
   d. What attitudes and language should we exhibit?
3. Read 1 Peter 3:8–12.
   a. How can your words or actions be an insult or a blessing to your husband?
   b. What are the character traits listed in verse 8? How are these traits in us a blessing to our husbands?
   c. What things must we do to love life and see good days?

Chapter 6

1. Read Proverbs 14:1.
   a. How does a wise woman build her house?
   b. How does the foolish woman tear it down?
   c. What are you currently doing that might be tearing your house down? What can you do to build it up?
2. Read Proverbs 11:29.
   a. How can we bring trouble to our family, especially concerning our attitudes toward our husband?
   b. How can we elevate our husband's status in the eyes of our children?
3. Read Ecclesiastes 4:9–12.
   a. What are the four images included in this passage?

    b. How does "two are better than one" relate to marriage?

    c. Give some specific examples of how you and your husband are stronger as a team than as individuals.

    d. In relationship to marriage, who could the third person in the cord be? (v. 12)

Chapter 7

1. Read Philippians 2:3–8.

    a. What attitude did Christ have concerning His relationship with mankind?

    b. How can we manifest this attitude in our marriage?

2. Read Psalm 101:5; Proverbs 8:13; 11:2; 16:18–19; 18:12; 21:4; 25:27; 29:23.

    a. What are some of the strong things God says about pride?

    b. How does pride play into the conflicts in your marriage?

3. Read Ephesians 2:10.

    a. How are we God's workmanship?

    b. What good works have you been prepared to do?

    c. How do you reflect those good works in the relationship with your husband?

4. Read through the Four Spiritual Laws in appendix 2.

    a. What thoughts come to your mind as you read them?

    b. Which circle (Law 4) best represents your life?

c. How does this affect your marriage?

Chapter 8

1. Read Ecclesiastes 2:17–23. Our culture worships success in business. The writer of Ecclesiastes offers another view.
   a. What does "the Preacher" (Eccl. 1:1 NASB) have to say about work?
   b. Why does he see his labor as meaningless?
   c. What has purpose in life?
2. Read Ecclesiastes 3:1–8.
   a. What does the Preacher say about the events of our life?
   b. How does this apply to your multifaceted life?
3. Read Proverbs 31:10–31. This passage refers to the character of an excellent wife.
   a. What are some of the tasks this woman is responsible for?
   b. What are some of the character traits emphasized by her actions?
   c. How is this relevant to your life?

Chapter 9

1. Read Isaiah 55:8–11 and Proverbs 2:1–8.
   a. Contrast God's thoughts to human thoughts.
   b. What are the benefits of God's wisdom?

2. Read Isaiah 48:17–18 and Isaiah 45:9–10.
   a. Explain the imagery in these verses.
   b. What are the implied warnings in these passages about not obeying God's Word?
3. Read Psalm 119:1–5 and Psalm 143:10.
   a. What is the attitude of the writer of these Psalms?
   b. What are the benefits of following God's Word?
4. Read Romans 12:2.
   a. What does our culture teach us about marriage?
   b. Why do we need to renew our minds in this area of thinking?

Chapter 10

1. Read Ephesians 5:22–24.
   a. What does submission mean to you?
   b. Why does God ask wives to submit to their husbands?
   c. What are the benefits of biblical submission?
2. Read Ephesians 5:33.
   a. How are submission and respect related?
   b. Why does God tell men to love their wives and women to respect their husbands?
   c. How can you show respect to your husband on a daily basis?

Appendix 2
The Four Spiritual Laws

By Bill Bright

JUST AS THERE are physical laws that govern the physical universe, so are there spiritual laws that govern your relationship with God.

LAW 1: *God **loves** you and offers a wonderful **plan** for your life.*

God's Love

"God so loved the world that he gave his one and only Son, that whoever believes in him shall not perish but have eternal life" (John 3:16 NIV).

God's Plan

[Christ speaking] "I came that they might have life, and might have it abundantly" [that it might be full and meaningful] (John 10:10).

Why is it that most people are not experiencing the abundant life? Because . . .

LAW 2: *Man is **sinful** and **separated** from God. Therefore, he cannot know and experience God's love and plan for his life.*

Man Is Sinful

"All have sinned and fall short of the glory of God" (Romans 3:23).

Man was created to have fellowship with God; but, because of his own stubborn self-will, he chose to go his own independent way and fellowship with God was broken. This self-will, characterized by an attitude of active rebellion or passive indifference, is an evidence of what the Bible calls sin.

Man Is Separated

"The wages of sin is death" [spiritual separation from God] (Romans 6:23).

This diagram illustrates that God is holy and man is sinful. A

great gulf separates the two. The arrows illustrate that man is continually trying to reach God and the abundant life through his own efforts, such as a good life, philosophy, or religion—but he inevitably fails.

The third law explains the only way to bridge this gulf . . .

LAW 3: *Jesus Christ is God's **only** provision for man's sin. Through Him you can know and experience God's love and plan for your life.*

He Died in Our Place

"God demonstrates His own love toward us, in that while we were yet sinners, Christ died for us" (Romans 5:8).

He Rose from the Dead

"Christ died for our sins . . . He was buried . . . He was raised on the third day, according to the Scriptures . . . He appeared to Peter, then to the twelve. After He appeared to more than five hundred . . ." (1 Corinthians 15:3–6).

He Is the Only Way to God

"Jesus said to him, 'I am the way, and the truth, and the life; no one comes to the Father, but through Me'" (John 14:6).

This diagram illustrates that God has bridged the gulf that

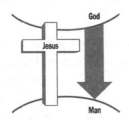

separates us from Him by sending His Son, Jesus Christ, to die on the cross in our place to pay the penalty for our sins.

It is not enough just to know these three laws . .

LAW 4: *We must individually **receive** Jesus Christ as Savior and*

Lord; then we can know and experience God's love and plan for our lives.

We Must Receive Christ

"As many as received Him, to them He gave the right to become children of God, even to those who believe in His name" (John 1:12).

We Receive Christ Through Faith

"By grace you have been saved through faith; and that not of yourselves, it is the gift of God; not as a result of works, that no one should boast" (Ephesians 2:8–9).

When We Receive Christ, We Experience a New Birth

(Read John 3:1–8.)

We Receive Christ Through Personal Invitation

[Christ speaking] "Behold, I stand at the door and knock; if anyone hears My voice and opens the door, I will come in to him" (Revelation 3:20).

Receiving Christ involves turning to God from self (repentance) and trusting Christ to come into our lives to forgive our sins and to make us what He wants us to be. Just to agree **intellectually** that Jesus Christ is the Son of God and that He died on the cross for our sins is not enough. Nor is it enough to have an **emotional** experience. We receive Jesus Christ by **faith**, as an act of the **will**.

These two circles represent two kinds of lives:

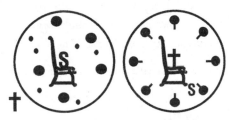

Self-Directed Life
S – Self is on the throne
† – Christ is outside the life
• – Interests are directed by self, often resulting in discord and frustration

Christ-Directed Life
† – Christ is in the life and on the throne
S – Self is yielding to Christ
• – Interests are directed by Christ, resulting in harmony with God's plan

Which circle best represents your life?

Which circle would you like to have represent your life?

The following explains how you can receive Christ:

You Can Receive Christ Right Now by Faith Through Prayer

(Prayer is talking with God.)

God knows your heart and is not so concerned with your words as He is with the attitude of your heart. The following is a suggested prayer:

Lord Jesus, I need You. Thank You for dying on the cross for my sins. I open the door of my life and receive You as my Savior and Lord. Thank You for forgiving my sins and giving me eternal life. Take control of the throne of my life. Make me the kind of person You want me to be.

Does this prayer express the desire of your heart?

If it does, I invite you to pray this prayer right now, and Christ will come into your life, as He promised.

How to Know That Christ Is in Your Life

Did you receive Christ into your life? According to His promise in Revelation 3:20, where is Christ right now in relation to you? Christ said that He would come into your life. Would He mislead you? On what authority do you know that God has answered your prayer? (The trustworthiness of God Himself and His Word.)

The Bible Promises Eternal Life to All Who Receive Christ

"God has given us eternal life, and this life is in His Son. He who has the Son has the life; he who does not have the Son of God does not have the life. These things I have written to you who believe in the name of the Son of God, in order that you may **know** that you have eternal life" (1 John 5:11–13).

Thank God often that Christ is in your life and that He will never leave you (Hebrews 13:5). You can know on the basis of His promise that Christ lives in you and that you have eternal life from the very moment you invite Him in. He will not deceive you.

An important reminder . . .

Do Not Depend on Feelings

The promise of God's Word, the Bible—not our feelings—is our authority. The Christian lives by faith (trust) in the trustworthiness of God Himself and His Word. This train diagram illustrates the relationship among **fact** (God and His Word), **faith** (our trust in God and His Word), and **feeling** (the result of our faith and obedience). (Read John 14:21.)

 The train will run with or without the caboose. However, it would be useless to attempt to pull the train by the caboose. In the same way, as Christians we do not depend on feelings or emotions, but we place our faith (trust) in the trustworthiness of God and the promises of His Word.

Now That You Have Received Christ

The moment you received Christ by faith, as an act of the will, many things happened, including the following:

Christ came into your life (Revelation 3:20; Colossians 1:27).

Your sins were forgiven (Colossians 1:14).

You became a child of God (John 1:12).

You received eternal life (John 5:24).

You began the great adventure for which God created you (John 10:10; 2 Corinthians 5:17; 1 Thessalonians 5:18).

Can you think of anything more wonderful that could happen to you than receiving Christ? Would you like to thank God in prayer right now for what He has done for you? By thanking God, you demonstrate your faith.

To enjoy your new life to the fullest . . .

Suggestions for Christian Growth

Spiritual growth results from trusting Jesus Christ. A life of faith will enable you to trust God increasingly with every detail of your life, and to practice the following:

G *Go* to God in prayer daily (John 15:7).
R *Read* God's Word daily (Acts 17:11); begin with the Gospel of John.
O *Obey* God moment by moment (John 14:21).
W *Witness* for Christ by your life and words (Matthew 4:19; John 15:8).
T *Trust* God for every detail of your life (1 Peter 5:7).
H *Holy Spirit*—allow Him to control and empower your daily life and witness (Galatians 5:16, 17; Acts 1:8; Ephesians 5:18).

Fellowship in a Good Church

God's Word instructs us not to forsake "the assembling of ourselves together" (Hebrews 10:25). Several logs burn brightly together, but put one aside on the cold hearth and the fire goes out. So it is with your relationship with other Christians.

If you do not belong to a church, do not wait to be invited. Take the initiative; call the pastor of a nearby church where Christ is honored and His Word is preached. Start this week, and make plans to attend regularly.

Acknowledgments

WHEN I FIRST mentioned the need for a book about sub-mission to my husband, I thought someone else would write it. Michael presented the idea to Greg Thornton, Senior Vice President of Moody Publishers, who liked the topic, but wanted me to write it. Thanks, Greg, for believing I had it in me.

I also want to thank Karen, Elsa, and Betsey who met with Michael, Greg Thornton, and me for a brainstorming session to discuss this idea. That meeting served as the frame-work for this project. Their enthusiasm and confidence in both the topic and my ability were overwhelming.

Thanks to Elizabeth Newenhuyse, my editor, who an-swered this publishing neophyte's abundant questions and whose encouraging words kept me going. Thanks, also, for the guts it took to agree to use the word "submission" in the title, even if it wasn't a popular idea at first.

Hanna, thanks for reading my first few chapters and pronouncing them "wonderful." Your smiles and tears as you read, and your words of affirmation, were more than I could have asked for.

Thanks to my Michael, Jessie, Devin, and Sarah, who encouraged me, and were willing to put up with late dinners and a dirty house on my more productive days.

Finally, thanks to all the godly women who let me ask uncomfortable questions and answered them with amazing vulnerability. Your insights into biblical submission and respect enhanced my understanding of my role in marriage. You are the ones who made this book possible.

And to my readers . . . thanks for picking up a book that was controversial and perhaps threatening. May God encourage you and mold you into His image as you follow His design for your marriage.

Now to Him who is able to keep you from stumbling, and to make you stand in the presence of His glory blameless with great joy, to the only God our Savior, through Jesus Christ our Lord, be glory, majesty, dominion and authority, before all time and now and forever. Amen.

Jude 24–25

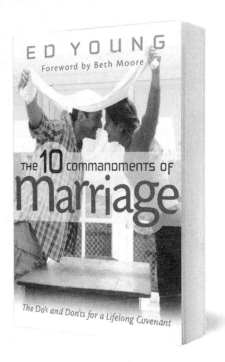

ISBN: 978-0-8024-3145-5

In words that are profound, often humorous, but always biblical, Ed Young draws from decades of counseling couples to provide ten commandments for a lifelong marriage that sizzles. God wants your marriage to be nothing short of incredible. And it could all begin with this amazing book.

by Ed Young

Find it now at your favorite local or online bookstore.

Sign up for Moody Publishers' Book Club on our website.

www.MoodyPublishers.com